SPOTLIGHT

C0-AVC-722

MARTHA'S VINEYARD

JEFF PERK

Contents

MARTHA'S VINEYARD

MARTHA'S VINEYARD

Forget about Martha—it's "The Vineyard" to everybody in the know, or simply "the Island" to those longtime residents who barely acknowledge the existence of nearby Nantucket. By any name, it's a peach: big enough to have quiet spots even in the busiest season, small enough that you can get to know it quickly, slightly more democratic than its neighbor in matters of room and board, and far more accessible to day-trippers. This is the island of seaside naps and lazy days in chaise lounges, of sailboats and bicycles, lighthouses and gingerbread cottages, artists and professors, carpenters and movie stars, presidential advisors and, occasionally, presidents. Water sports, historical exhibits, and nature trails provide alternatives to the beach, while abundant seafood and all manner of sweets lay to rest that austere summer diet you fleetingly considered in order to fit into last year's swimsuit.

The Vineyard's 100-plus square miles are neatly divisible into "up-island" and "down-island." As on Cape Cod, this holdover from days of whalers and sailors makes sense if you remember that degrees of longitude ascend from east to west.

Down-island is the Vineyard's pedestrian-friendly threshold: Vineyard Haven, Oak Bluffs, and Edgartown. Along with a near monopoly on knickknack shops, sweet treats, and Black Dog T-shirts, down-island is where good food, nightlife, and accommodations are all within walking distance of each other. Car-free visitors also have the flexibility of catching a ferry at almost a moment's notice. While you are more likely to find the comforting glow of streetlights rather

HIGHLIGHTS

◖ Oak Bluffs Campground: Stroll curvy lanes amid a postcard-perfect collection of colorful Victorian gingerbread cottages (page 28).

◖ Historic Downtown Edgartown: Stately waterfront mansions and a stunning Greek Revival church frame the charming shop-filled blocks and narrow garden-lined lanes of the island's oldest town (page 38).

◖ Edgartown Lighthouse: Beautiful harbor and town views await at both the beach around the base and the railed deck at the top of this historic 45-foot tower a short stroll from downtown (page 39).

◖ Sailing Katama Bay: Water rats know nothing is half so much worth doing as messing about in boats, a maxim proven doubly true when lolling under sail aboard one of the Vineyard's beautiful windjammers or wooden yachts (page 45).

◖ Mytoi: The serenity of a Japanese-style landscaped garden provides an oasis amid the pines of rural Chappaquiddick (page 46).

◖ Wasque Point and Cape Poge: Swim, surf-cast, kayak, bird-watch, take tours to a remote lighthouse, or do nothing but lay listening to the steady beat of the Atlantic Ocean upon miles of barrier beach (page 47).

◖ Gay Head Cliffs: Watching the sunset from the upper edge of this many-shaded clay scarp is rivaled only by trekking amid the mussel-fringed boulders, mermaid purses, and other marine curiosities fetched up along the rough shore at its base (page 56).

◖ Long Point Wildlife Refuge: Comb the beach, let the strong surf scour your summer cares away, take a paddle tour of Tisbury Great Pond, or just saunter through the heaths of this ecologically rare coastal sandplain grasslands (page 60).

◖ Cedar Tree Neck: Easy trails through a varied woodland habitat lead to a beautiful scenic shore along Vineyard Sound (page 61).

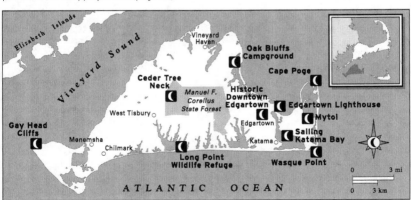

LOOK FOR **◖** TO FIND RECOMMENDED SIGHTS, ACTIVITIES, DINING, AND LODGING.

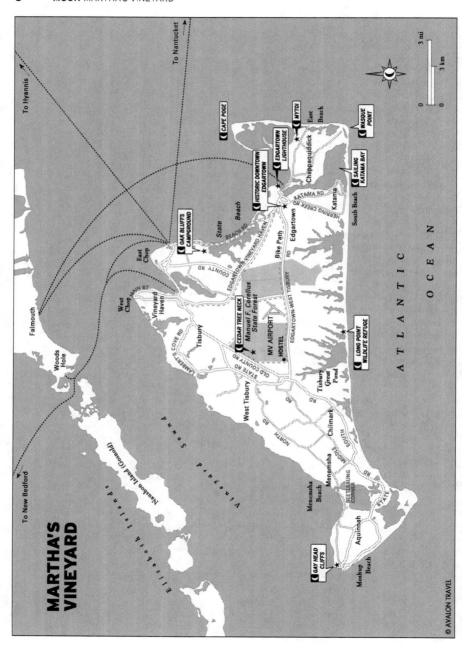

MARTHA'S VINEYARD

To Hyannis

To Nantucket

To New Bedford

Falmouth

Woods Hole

Elizabeth Islands

Naushon Island (Gosnold)

Vineyard Sound

CAPE POGE

EDGARTOWN LIGHTHOUSE

MYTOI

HISTORIC DOWNTOWN EDGARTOWN

East Beach

WASQUE POINT

Chappaquiddick

SAILING KATAMA BAY

KATAMA RD

Katama

South Beach

Beach

HERRING CREEK RD

OAK BLUFFS CAMPGROUND

State

BEACH RD

Bike Path

Edgartown

East Chop

EDGARTOWN-VINEYARD HAVEN RD

West Chop

EDGARTOWN-WEST TISBURY RD

Vineyard Haven

CEDAR TREE NECK

Manuel F. Correllus State Forest

MV AIRPORT

HOSTEL

Tisbury

MAIN ST

LAMBERT'S COVE RD

STATE RD

OLD COUNTY RD

LONG POINT WILDLIFE REFUGE

Tisbury Great Pond

West Tisbury

NORTH RD

MIDDLE RD

SOUTH RD

STATE RD

Chilmark

Menemsha

BEETLEBUNG CORNER

Menemsha Beach

Aquinnah

GAY HEAD CLIFFS

Moshup Beach

ATLANTIC OCEAN

0   3 mi
0   3 km

© AVALON TRAVEL

than a chorus of crickets outside your bedroom window at night, down-island offers plenty of scenic beauty and is home to more than half of the Vineyard's two dozen public beaches.

Up-island is the island's southwestern corner farthest from the Cape Cod ferries. It comprises the predominantly rural towns of West Tisbury, Chilmark, and Aquinnah, home to only a smattering of small restaurants, stores, and galleries. Many of the area's undulating country roads are lined by great allées of oak, like antebellum plantation driveways, and the woods are filled with the drystone walls of bygone sheep farms. The up-island hills—the Vineyard's highest ground—offer great views en route to their abrupt tumble into the sea beneath the steady sweep of the beacon in redbrick Gay Head Light.

While even this section of the Vineyard heavily depends on "summer people," it also relies on agriculture and fishing. Its working roots are especially visible in picturesque Menemsha harbor—home to more groundfish draggers and lobster trappers than luxury yachts—and at the seasonal biweekly farmers' market in West Tisbury. To experience up-island at its best generally requires owning or renting a set of wheels (two or four), although every town is linked to down-island throughout the year by public transit.

HISTORY
Early Visitors

Martha's Vineyard is generally said to take its name from an abundance of native wild grapes and the daughter of Bartholomew Gosnold, the English captain who spent the late spring of 1602 around Buzzards Bay and the Elizabeth Islands (which he named in honor of his Queen), in what was then known as "the North part of Virginia." However, given that Gosnold didn't have a daughter named Martha and that his mother-in-law, Martha Goulding, helped finance his voyage, it is more plausible he was honoring her. According to the "Briefe and true Relation" of the voyage, by one of its members, John Brereton, Gosnold actually applied "Marthaes

THE LEGEND OF MOSHUP

(As told by Thomas Cooper, Gay Head Indian, to Englishman Benjamin Basset in 1792)

The first Indian who came to the Vineyard, was brought thither with his dog on a cake of ice. When he came to Gay Head, he found a very large man, whose name was Moshup. He had a wife and five children, four sons and one daughter; and lived in the Den [Gay Head's circular depression]. He used to catch whales, and then pluck up trees, and make a fire, and roast them. The coals of the trees, and the bones of the whales, are now to be seen. After he was tired of staying here, he told his children to go and play ball on a beach that joined Noman's Land to Gay Head. He then made a mark with his toe across the beach at each end, and so deep, that the water followed, and cut away the beach; so that his children were in fear of drowning. They took their sister up, and held her out of the water. He told them to act as if they were going to kill whales; and they were all turned into killers [killer whales]. The sister was dressed in large stripes. He gave them strict charge always to be kind to her. His wife mourned the loss of her children so exceedingly, that he threw her away. She fell upon Seconet [Sakonnet Point, RI], near the rocks, where she lived some time, exacting contribution of all who passed by water. After a while she was changed into a stone. The entire shape remained for many years. But after the English came, some of them broke off the arms, head, &c. but most of the body remains to this day. Moshup went away nobody knows whither. He had no conversation with the Indians, but was kind to them, by sending whales, &c. ashore to them to eat. But after they grew thick around him he left them.

(Simmons, William S., Spirit of the New England Tribes)

vineyard" to a very small, uninhabited island overgrown with various fruit-bearing shrubs and such "an incredible store of Vines...that we could not goe for treading upon them." Probably this was what's now aptly called Noman's Land, a naval gunnery-range-turned-wildlife-sanctuary off Aquinnah's south shore. By 1610, cartographers assigned the name to the much larger adjacent island. There it remains today, having outlasted "Capawack" (probably from the Algonquian word for harbor, *kuppaug*), which was for decades the most widely used appellation of the first English settlers.

The lure for Gosnold, as for other captains who ranged the New England coast in the early 17th century, was sassafras. The safrole in the leaves is now known to be a carcinogen, but to Gosnold's contemporaries the plant was widely believed to be a cure-all. "The roote of sassafras hath power to comfort the liver," enthused one 1597 herbal encyclopedia, "and to dissolve oppilations, to comfort the weake and feeble stomacke, to cause a good appetite, to consume windiness, the chiefest cause of cruditie and indigestion, stay vomiting, and make sweete a stinking breath." Perhaps more important to the gentlemen of Europe—whose demand for the stuff kept the price (and profit margins) so high—was the belief that it could cure "the French Poxe" (i.e. syphilis).

They Came, They Saw, They Converted

When Gosnold's ship, *The Concord*, anchored in local waters, the Vineyard was well inhabited by Native Americans related to the Wampanoags of coastal Massachusetts and Rhode Island—a federation of Algonquian-speaking bands whose ancestors had occupied *Noe-pe* (the land "amid the waters") for at least 9,000 years. The 17th-century Wampanoags were farmers and fishermen organized in close-knit villages around *sachems* (hereditary leaders) and *pauwaus* (religious leaders and physicians, or medicine men). When the first white settlers arrived, in 1642, four sachems presided over the island's estimated population of 3,000.

These first immigrants were farmers and shepherds from the Boston area led by Thomas Mayhew, Jr., a missionary, and his father, a merchant. For 40 pounds and a beaver hat (about three times the price allegedly paid for Manhattan 15 years earlier), Mayhew, Sr., had purchased from the Earl of Stirling the patent to all islands then unoccupied by the English off the south shore of Cape Cod—and, importantly, beyond the boundaries of both the existing Pilgrim and Puritan colonies. Bypassing the sandy heaths of Nantucket and the too-small Elizabeth Islands as ill suited to the homesteading needs of their party, the Mayhews settled on the Vineyard.

The Wampanoags accepted them, despite previous experience that included an English captain's kidnapping a sachem for zoolike display in London. Mayhew, Sr., assured the Indians that his master, King James, though superior to their sachems, "would in no measure invade their Jurisdictions." Surprisingly, he kept his word, paying for property rights as his settlements expanded or—as in the case of Nantucket—before he resold possessions granted him under his original royal patent.

Such honesty merits special mention because it stands out so much from the shameless deceits of Mayhew's mainland contemporaries, but tolerance may have begun as a form of détente. The Wampanoags could not have forgotten the ruinous Pequot War, ended just five years before, and the devastation it brought that tribe in nearby coastal Connecticut for getting in the way of the English. And Mayhew's thirty-odd homesteaders would have been conscious of being far from the assistance of authorities in either the Massachusetts Bay or Plymouth colonies.

In any event, the Indians' mortality rate and acculturation made hostilities or illegal land grabs wholly unnecessary. Beginning with a nasty plague outbreak a few years after the settlers' arrival, European diseases reduced the Wampanoag population by over 70 percent within as many years. Devoted missionary work by both Mayhews (capitalizing in part on the *pauwaus'* inability to stem disease-related deaths) converted many more Indians into model subjects of English law. Some were so thoroughly assimilated that the English islanders paid to send them to Harvard to be trained for the ministry.

After Mayhew, Jr., was lost at sea on a fundraising trip to England, Mayhew, Sr., effectively ran the island as the private Manor of Tisbury, with himself as Lord and Chief Justice. Intolerant of dissent, the Governor-for-Life jailed or exiled his fellow landowners as he saw fit, until finally succumbing to nature's term limits at the age of 85. Nine years of squabbling later, in 1691, the Vineyard was annexed to the new Province of Massachusetts formed by monarchs William and Mary after the various colonial charters were revoked by an English parliament impatient with their subjects' unruliness.

Population Pressures

Frothy politics aside, the remainder of the 17th century and most of the 18th were marked most by rapid population growth among whites—more from new births than new immigrants. Predictably, this had side effects. When J. Hector de Crèvecoeur wrote, in his *Letters from an American Farmer,* that travelers to the Vineyard couldn't avoid becoming acquainted with all its principal families, he was complimenting island hospitality, but he might as well have been satirizing the islanders' inbreeding. At the time of his visit, in the 1770s, almost every new island marriage was between cousins of some kind; by the mid-1800s, half the island's population had one of only a dozen surnames. Until settlement by off-islanders in the 20th century introduced new blood (and disapproval of marriage between cousins), there was no stigma attached to the high incidence of deafness among newborns—particularly in the rural up-island towns. Until after World War I, not surprisingly, sign language was widely spoken here.

The most pressing problem posed by the high birth rate, though, was that, like an infestation of weevils in a small garden, people proceeded to strip their patrimony bare, forc-

ing a shift from sheep-shears, milking stools, and plowshares to oars, nets, and harpoons. Turning from their deforested, overgrazed hills (and later from an economy completely KO'd by English raids and embargoes during the American Revolution), an estimated 20 percent of the Vineyard's men—Wampanoag and white alike—became expert whalers and merchant seamen, as highly prized by captains and ship owners as their Nantucket brethren. "Go where you will from Nova Scotia to the Mississippi," wrote de Crèvecoeur, "you will find almost everywhere some natives of these two islands employed in seafaring occupations."

But this didn't last, either. By the 1840s, local whale-oil merchants faced stiff competition from mainland producers (who were closer to their consumers), and local wool producers were edged out by cheaper foreign imports. In the year of John Brown's pre–Civil War raid on the federal arsenal at Harpers Ferry, whale-oil prices were shot down by cheaper Pennsylvania crude; by the end of the war, the whale fleet had been scrapped, sunk, or was rotting at the wharves. The Vineyard's whaling days were over.

"We'll Camp Awhile in the Wilderness"

As seafaring fortunes waned, the newest and most lasting transformation of the Vineyard was taking root in the Second Great Awakening, a nationwide resurgence of Methodist revivalism. In 1835, southern New England Methodists began holding revival tent meetings in an oak-shaded meadow they christened Wesleyan Grove, erecting a small village of huge "society tents" each August to house the crowds who came to experience a week of Bible-thumping preaching and religious conversion. The year the market for whale oil nosedived, 1859, some 12,000 souls turned up at the camp meeting, seeking salvation in 400 tents.

These tent revivals were such a magnet for tourists that they were featured in the *New York Times* travel section and in illustrated weeklies such as *Harper's.* The great congregation-sponsored tents were gradually replaced

VINEYARD ETIQUETTE

The list of past and present Vineyard residents includes Spike Lee, Harvey Weinstein, Mike Wallace, Carly Simon, Denzel Washington, Alan Dershowitz, Judy Blume, Diane Sawyer, David Letterman, James Taylor, Bill Murray, Walter Cronkite, Art Buchwald, John Belushi, and Jackie O. Maybe the sun does shine a little brighter on these people, but don't come to the Vineyard expecting to bask in it yourself.

Local wisdom holds that the Vineyard attracts celebrities precisely because locals have either too much Yankee sense or Puritan humility to make a fuss over cultural icons in the flesh. This legendary discretion has become the cornerstone of Vineyard etiquette, which declares that celebrities are to be allowed to go about unmolested by photographers or autograph-seekers. Should you see Somebody, you should feign indifference instead of, say, crossing the street to get a better look. If Somebody sits at the next table in a restaurant, you are requested to act nonchalant instead of playing paparazzo with your camera.

You can do otherwise, of course, but then many trees' worth of *Vineyard Gazette* newsprint will be expended by local vigilantes clucking their tongues over another tourist who "just doesn't get it." Anyway, you're wasting your time driving Chilmark's back roads hoping to catch some box-office headliners shmoozing over a barbecue; most of those Very Important People stay so well out of sight that the closest you'll get is the airport, within earshot of their chartered jets.

by fanciful wooden family cottages whose occupants soon set aside as much time for parlor entertainment, croquet, and promenading along the seashore as for hymns, gospel, and prayer. A speculative group of investors, the Oak Bluffs Land and Wharf Company, began constructing a summer resort around Wesleyan Grove, deliberately mirroring the camp meeting grounds' informality, capitalizing on the impeccable reputation and high moral character of the revival gathering (as opposed to the liquor-soaked haven of high society across Vineyard Sound at Newport) and targeting the same sober Christians as the camp meetings. Out of this emerging middle class of shopkeepers, blacksmiths, carpenters, watchmakers, and other artisans seeking both a hard-earned reprieve from sweltering cities and safe recreation for their families, "Cottage City"—eventually renamed Oak Bluffs—was born.

Over the last century, the Vineyard has continued to cultivate its reputation as a summer resort, although the demographics of both the visitors and their hosts have changed. The 1960s and '70s saw a rise in VW owners and McGovern voters coming to roost here permanently, accompanied by a handful of celebrities looking for a place to avoid the limelight. Both have been followed by the seasonal tide of college students seeking good parties and a wave of professionals, academics, and business execs on a spree of second-home buying. These days, media moguls and A-list movie stars are plunking down millions for secluded beachfronts and pedigreed estates. Besides sending high-end property values toward the moon, this latest trend has drawn stargazers who either don't know or don't care about the local etiquette. Old-timers may rightly wonder whether the "good and happy grocer" of the camp meeting years would see the Vineyard of today as the piece of heaven he had sought or the profligate high-rolling resort he had sought to escape. But if you weren't here in the mellow hippie years, you have nothing to mourn. Local letter-to-the-editor writers may perennially wring their hands over the changes, but until all the old stone walls crumble to dust and the lighthouses fall into the seas, there will be enough uniquely New England flavor here to keep comparisons with Vail, Sun Valley, or Beverly Hills firmly at bay.

PLANNING YOUR TIME

Although the Vineyard is in New England, instead of four seasons to the year there are just two: in-season and off-season. The first is the big mixed-blessing phenomenon of the summer, which has carried the Vineyard economy now for more than a century. It's a fairly well-rehearsed course: After a practice gallop over the Memorial Day weekend, *in-season* does a few light warm-up laps through June before finally bolting out of the gate in a breakneck frenzy on the Fourth of July. Careening like a tornado through Labor Day, it finally slows to a canter by Columbus Day—the semiofficial end of the race and the point at which most owners retire to tally up their winnings.

Lingering momentum and clement weather can prop up *off-season* weekends through Thanksgiving, but then the island finally becomes again the property of its year-round residents, who savor the calm until their memory of the last blockbuster summer becomes so distant that they grow impatient for the sequel. (Not all locals cope well with the annual shift from traffic jams to cabin fever: the drought–flood–drought resort economy, coupled with intense isolation, is believed to strongly contribute to the high local incidence of alcoholism.)

The biggest difference between in-season and off-season is, as you might expect, a sudden increase in the availability of just about everything. By the same token, it's also at this point that the restaurants, buses, ferries, accommodations, and shops all start to scale back their operating hours. Beach buses and hourly public shuttles between up- and down-island are the first to cease, stopping promptly after Labor Day weekend, not to resume until the following mid- to late June (the shuttles still run, but not nearly as often). By mid-October, most up-island restaurants and half the B&Bs in West Tisbury, Chilmark, and Aquinnah have followed suit. By autumn, down-island towns start to roll up the rugs, cover the furniture, and forward the mail, too—but they have enough year-round resi-

cottages that formed the original town of Oak Bluffs

dents to at least keep a few restaurants open all year. Last, but not least, there's Vineyard Haven; thanks to four-season Steamship service, it actually retains a passing resemblance to a fully functioning small town, even at the nadir of winter.

The off-season brings with it certain requirements—double-check restaurant hours, for example, and rely more on driving than you would in the longer and warmer days of summer. But these are more than outweighed by advantages such as choosing lodgings upon arrival (rather than sight-unseen three months in advance) and dining when ready, without waiting in line for an hour or making do with a fifth-choice reservation. While the *early* off-season (Apr.–June) is most prized, anyone looking for a cozy weekend escape to an austere Winslow Homer landscape shouldn't rule out December, or even February.

What you should *not* expect from the off-season in the Vineyard is significant savings. Innkeepers' supply costs are as high in winter as in summer, and off-season business is too sparse to be worth a price war. Yes, some room rates may drop almost 50 percent between summer and winter, but that simply reflects the fact that July prices are stratospheric; they return in January to the realm of the average Marriott hotel.

Like resort destinations all over the country, the Vineyard struggles with the pressures of popularity. Realtors talk about three-acre minimum lots as the balm for fears of over-development, but look closely as you come in on the ferry from Woods Hole and you'll see what land conservationists are concerned about—the wooded Vineyard shore is filling with rooftops. The development issue grows ever more urgent as summer traffic in down-island towns approaches your average metropolitan rush-hour gridlock. You can be part of the solution rather than the problem by leaving your car on the mainland if at all possible, and taking advantage of the year-round public transit, extensive bike paths, taxis, and your feet.

Those using foreign currency must make their cash exchanges prior to arriving—none of the banks here handle such transactions. You won't ever be far from an automated teller machine in the down-island towns, but up-island is a different story—beyond Beetlebung Corner, there's nothing, so come prepared.

Vineyard Haven

This is the island's largest year-round community and only year-round ferry port. But by all appearances, it's just your average small seaside town of about 2,000 stalwart souls, with a little light industry near the wharf, tree-shaded residential streets overlooking the harbor, and a small commercial downtown. White clapboard and gray shingle descendants of the venerable, sharp-gabled, Cape-style house rub shoulders with old captains' mansions. The automotive spectrum ranges from rust-flecked American sedans to teenagers in their parents' hand-me-down foreign imports, from oversized pickup trucks that clearly earn their mudflaps to mirror-polished SUVs. Whatever its varied occupations the rest of the year, come summer, the town has its hands full playing host and maître d' to the million-plus visitors swarming through it.

Once known by the Wampanoags as "Nobnocket" (place by the pond), the port was known to later generations of sailors as Holmes Hole, after a 17th-century landowner. Early in the Victorian era, image-conscious citizens changed the name after deciding they preferred living in a place that sounded closer to heaven than hell. Since then, the harborside village has grown indistinguishable from Tisbury, the 17th-century township of which it was once just a part—but, aside from legal documents and town stationery, both general usage and the U.S. Postal Service now favor "Vineyard Haven" for the whole.

Visitors disgorged by the ferries will find restaurants, shops, accommodations, car and bike rentals, ATMs, and (in the Steamship Authority Terminal beside the pier and, seasonally, above the Stop & Shop parking lot across the street) public restrooms—all within a few blocks' walk. The one amenity you needn't bother looking for is a liquor store; by law, Vineyard Haven, like all the up-island towns, is dry.

SIGHTS
Historic Architecture
Since "the Great Fire of 1883" destroyed its center, the town's oldest buildings are found on upper Main Street north of the Bank of Martha's Vineyard building (whose distinctive facade, a cross between Craftsman-style stone and Mediterranean tile bungalow, occupies the grounds of the harness shop where the fire may have begun) and a block farther up from the harbor along William Street. Many of the fifty-odd houses included in the Historic District along this quiet street were built as a result of

the whaling and trade industries. Befitting the wealth of their builders, some of these houses typify the Greek Revival style now most commonly associated with old banks.

Plenty of New England's most attractive civic architecture has been inspired as much by religion as commercial profit, as some of this town's present and former churches attest. Tucked along side streets crossing Williams are three worthy examples: the classically inspired **Tisbury Town Hall,** a former Congregational and Baptist Church on Spring Street that's also known as Association Hall; the newer United Methodist **Stone Church,** on Church Street, built early this century to replace its demonstrably flammable predecessor; and, opposite, the former 1833 Methodist meetinghouse, now **The Vineyard Playhouse,** the island's only professional theater. Association Hall is also home to a performance center, the **Katharine Cornell Memorial Theater,** a fully accessible space used by various local groups. During Town Hall's regular business hours it's worth stepping inside the theater for a peek at the large island-themed murals by the late Stan Murphy, a Vineyard artist known for his luminous paintings of people and nature.

West Chop

Vineyard Haven's V-shaped harbor is protected on either side by jaw-like hunks of land known as East and West Chop. Upper Main Street runs along West Chop to a separate village of Tisbury, located at the end; East Chop belongs to neighboring Oak Bluffs.

About two miles up Main from the downtown shops is the 19th-century **West Chop Lighthouse,** sitting beside the road for photographers' convenience, though not open to the public (it's a private Coast Guard residence). The current 1891 brick tower is the third incarnation in a series of lights at this location that have guided seafarers since James Monroe sat in the White House. The white beacon, visible on the mainland, shows red if you get too close to the shoals off the end of the point.

West Chop Park, near the turnaround loop at the end of Main, is favored for watching the

© KATHRYN OSGOOD

view of Vineyard Haven Harbor

ISLAND TOURS

Want to start off your Vineyard holiday with a 2.5-hour narrated trip around all six towns? The white, pink, and turquoise old school buses of **Martha's Vineyard Sightseeing,** a.k.a. Island Transport (508/627-8687, www.mvtour.com, $26 adults, $14 kids 12 and under), rendezvous with all incoming ferries in both Vineyard Haven and Oak Bluffs 9 A.M.–4 P.M. daily mid-May–late October, and with the 10:30 and 11:30 A.M. ferries from April 15–November 1. You can buy your tickets at the Steamship Authority terminal in Woods Hole, or aboard the Hy-Line, Falmouth, and New Bedford ferries en route to the island.

The all-island buses pay only a cursory visit to the down-island towns, since the vehicles are too large to negotiate narrow downtown streets, but they do include a 25-minute stop at the Aquinnah Cliffs. The tour guides are typically off-island college students whose knowledge of the Vineyard comes from scripts, so when it comes to identifying celebrity driveways or explaining what happened at Chappaquiddick in 1969, take what they say with a good dash of salt.

Alternatively, consider taking a walking tour with a real historian. **Vineyard History Tours** (508/627-2529, $12, free to kids under 12) conducts a "Ghosts, Gossip, and Downright Scandal" 75-minute tour in each of the down-island towns – Vineyard Haven, Oak Bluffs, and Edgartown – typically two or three times a week in season as well as by appointment year-round. Call for current departure times and starting points.

sunsets over Vineyard Sound, but any time on a clear day, it offers a nice view out over what was once one of the world's busiest coastal waterways. Before railroads and the 1914 completion of the Cape Cod Canal siphoned away most of the cargo and passengers, this area was second only to the English Channel in boat traffic. Two hundred years ago, you could have counted scores of sails belonging to coastwise packets bound for Boston or New York and merchant vessels bearing West Indies molasses, South American hides, Sumatran spices, and Arabian coffee. Until technology enabling precise calculation of a ship's longitude became widely available, in the 19th century, most "East-Indiamen" put in at Vineyard Haven or Woods Hole before negotiating the great extended hook of Cape Cod; to set a course for Boston or Salem directly from the Caribbean or South Atlantic would have otherwise risked a fatal snag on Nantucket South Shoals.

ENTERTAINMENT

A variety of groups keep the performing arts alive on the island, often in casual surroundings such as local churches and school auditoriums. Professional theater, however, does have a home of its own: **The Vineyard Playhouse** (10 Church St., box office 508/696-6300, Oct.–June 508/693-6450, www.vineyardplayhouse .org) presents some half-dozen mostly contemporary works by mostly American playwrights on the main stage between late June and Labor Day (performances 8 P.M. Tues.–Sun.), followed by such perennial off-season events as a fall new-play competition, a winter holiday show, and a spring short-play festival. Rush tickets and previews of all shows are sharply discounted, so if you happen to catch an early dinner in town, it's a cinch to stroll by after and see if there's a pair of good seats left for dessert.

The Playhouse also stages Shakespeare in the outdoor **Tisbury Amphitheater,** near the corner of West Spring Street and State Road, beside beautiful Lake Tashmoo, in July and August (5 P.M. Wed.–Sun., $15), weather permitting.

Named after the local resident and Broadway star whose philanthropy made it possible, nearby **Katharine Cornell Memorial Theater** (51 Spring St.) in Vineyard Haven's Association Hall hosts community theater and chamber music. Consult the island papers or check the display case in front of the building to find out what's currently going on.

The home of the summer blockbuster is the intimate **Capawock Theater** (Main St.,

508/627-6689), one of the island's two year-round cinemas showing first-run features and occasional foreign films. Truly independent arthouse fare—anything with subtitles, documentaries, and favorites from the Sundance/Cannes festival circuit—is screened on a regular basis throughout the year at the Katherine Cornell Memorial Theater on Spring Street by the **Silver Screen Film Society** (www.mv filmsociety.com). Schedules are always listed in the weekly papers.

The eclectic side of the local music scene can be heard live on Saturday nights at **Che's Lounge** (38C Main St., 508/693-8555, year-round), or at their weekly open mic on Wednesday. Che's also features regular poetry slams and weekly salsa dancing (lessons provided).

The Vineyard's creative community includes plenty of writers, poets, and scholars who take to the bully pulpit of the Vineyard Haven Public Library (200 Main St., 508/696-4211, www.vhlibrary.org) on a fairly regular basis, or pop up for the occasional reading at Bunch of Grapes bookstore. The weekly calendar section of the *Martha's Vineyard Times* (www.mvtimes .com) is the best resource for specific announcements of such upcoming events.

SHOPPING

An abundance of craftspeople and commercial artists consider the Vineyard their year-round home, and Vineyard Haven has its fair share of galleries displaying their work. It has also become the island's center for home furnishings, with an eclectic collection of retailers offering very personal visions of how to beautify your nest, from kilims to English country antiques. There are unique specialty stores, too—aromatherapy potions here, Native American jewelry there—and enough apparel shops to keep a clotheshorse occupied for hours. No need to shop on an empty stomach, either—you can grab a quick sandwich or snack around almost every corner.

One of the first sights to greet passengers disembarking from the Woods Hole ferry is **The Black Dog Bakery** (11 Water St., 508/693-

4786, www.theblackdog.com, 5:30 A.M.–6 P.M. daily), across from the Stop & Shop Market. Although the muffins seem to have shrunk in proportion to their popularity, the Dog is still a mighty contender in the island's baked goods sweepstakes. The related tavern on the beach behind the bakery was famous even before President Clinton and family stopped in for a bite while vacationing here in the '90s, but the place now seems determined to clothe half the planet in its trademark T-shirts—which is why part of the bakery may at first glance resemble a sportswear store. If you're interested in seeing what, besides clothing, the owners have chosen to put their logo on, from black lab dinnerware to paw-print drawer pulls, stop in at the **General Store** (508/696-8182, 9 A.M.–5 P.M. daily, off-season hours vary) behind the bakery. If you manage to somehow escape Vineyard Haven without paying this place a visit, don't worry—like an increasing number of other island retailers, the Black Dog General Store has branches in all three down-island towns.

Opposite the Black Dog Tavern, on the dead-end lane headed toward the harbor, is **Stina Sayre Design** (13 Beach St. Ext., 508/560-1011, www.stinasayre.com, year-round by appointment or chance), a small atelier of women's couture. If you're on the island around Thanksgiving you can catch Sayre's annual fashion show at the Mansion House, but she welcomes drop-ins, too, as she enjoys meeting potential clients in person.

The very presence of **The Devil's Dictionary** (9 Main St., 508/693-0372, 10 A.M.–10 P.M. Mon.–Sat., noon–7 P.M. Sun. mid-June–mid-Sept., off-season hours vary, closed Feb.–Mar.) on Main Street is one of those defiant gestures proving that the Vineyard is not just your parent's family resort. Barware, cigar-smoking accessories, pin-up calendars, pool- and poker-playing necessities, leather gameboards, and assorted gadgets are among its "defining products for men." There is also a smokers' club in the back complete with pool table, plus hookahs and loose tobacco for all you louche Paul Bowles wannabes.

Decorative wares of subtle beauty fill **Nochi**

(29 Main St., 508/693-9074, www.nochimv .com, 10 A.M.–5 P.M. Mon.–Sat. Apr.–Dec.), from fine table and bed linens to distressed furniture. European ceramics, selected clothing for women, French soaps, and fresh flowers round out the many items of interest, but this shop is also noteworthy for carrying the delectable and inspired confections of Vosges Haut-Chocolat *and* Mariebelle, two of America's outstanding boutique chocolate makers.

Worth a detour down at the end of the little courtyard across the street from Nochi is the flagstone-floor studio of local artist **Richard Lee** (behind 34 Main St., 508/693-4156). His hallucinogenic style of reverse painting on glass is whimsically zoomorphic—imagine the Ramayana illustrated by Hieronymus Bosch and you'll get the idea. He also paints and gilds animal skulls and furniture. If, as is often the case, Richard is out enjoying summer at the beach rather than laboring over his workbench, a great spot to relax and bid your time waiting for him is **Che's Lounge** (38C Main St., 508/693-8555, noon–7 P.M. Sun.–Mon., noon–9 P.M. Fri.–Sat. year-round) just opposite, a coffeehouse-cum-hangout par excellence, with excellent teas, chai, and of course coffee, plus mighty fine baked goods from the Scottish Bakehouse on State Road.

The **Shaw Cramer Gallery** (76 Main St., 508/696-7323, www.shawcramergallery .com, 10 A.M.–5 P.M. daily May–mid-Oct., hours vary Oct.–Apr.) is the place to go to put some serious pizzazz into your dinnerware or furnishings; among the functional and decorative contemporary housewares are locally made pillowcases.

Quite the retro blend of new, old, and new reproductions of the old are found at **Mix** (65 Main St., 508/693-8240, 9:30 A.M.–6 P.M. Sun.–Mon., 9:30 A.M.–7 P.M. Fri.–Sat. July 4–early Sept.; 10 A.M.–5 P.M. daily the rest of the year), a store that more than lives up to its name. There are trays made from recycled magazines, hula-girl highball glasses, antique cameras, vintage diner signage, and whimsical onesies and other baby clothing. There's colorful melamine and acrylic tabletop goods from

Precidio (the Canadian company that brings you Rachael Ray's line of hipster products), sake sets cast from Limoge porcelain, and a broad line of quality ceramics by Mud Australia, as well as quilts, scarves, sunhats, and floor mats, canisters of gourmet loose teas, and first-edition Golden Books for kids. The gift possibilities are, as you can see, virtually endless.

Turn down the lane beside Bowl & Board to find **Midnight Farm** (Cromwell Ln., 508/693-1997, www.midnightfarm.net, 9 A.M.–9 P.M. Mon.–Sat. and 10 A.M.–6 P.M. Sun. late May–Aug., 9:30 A.M.–5:30 P.M. Mon.–Sat. and 10 A.M.–5 P.M. Sun. the rest of the year), widely known as Carly Simon's store, although she's just one of the business partners. It's full of very beautiful and very expensive art, housewares, barefoot-in-the-park casual clothing, eco-friendly personal care products, and one-of-a-kind tchotchkes.

If $80 scarves or $2,000 hand-finished wooden sideboards aren't in your budget, there's always the **Thrift Store** (38 Lagoon Pond Rd., 508/693-2278, www.mvcommuni tyservices.com, 9 A.M.–5 P.M. Mon.–Fri. and 9 A.M.–2 P.M. Sat.–Sun.) between Island Color and Tisbury Printers, a block from the post office. Some surprisingly high-quality merchandise has been known to turn up on the racks amid all the old record albums, used clothing, and household jetsam, making shopping there a little like playing the lottery.

As a port of some renown, Vineyard Haven has the usual complement of marine-related services on Beach Road around the many boat repair shops. It isn't all outboard motors and anti-fouling paint, though, as illustrated by the flea-market array of consignment material at **Pyewacket's Flea Circus** (63 Beach Rd., 508/696-7766), in the yellow clapboard house between the shipyards and the Tisbury Market Place mini-mall.

If you paid attention to the upper stories of the downtown streetscape, you probably noticed the pterodactyl weathervane adorning the building opposite the Bank of Martha's Vineyard on Main. That little woman grasped in the dinosaur's talons is, of course, Raquel

Welch, but if you remember the '60s cult classic *One Million Years B.C.*, you already knew that. If you wonder where that 'vane came from—and whether you can get one like it—head to the studio-cum-gallery of **Tuck & Holand Metal Sculptors,** about 10 minutes' walk out of town along State Road (275 State Rd., 508/693-3914, www.tuckand holand.com, 9 A.M.–5 P.M. daily). There's about a two-year waiting list for the firm's unique *repoussé* (French for "pushed from the back," referring to how they're made, not how they work) weathervanes, which sell for prices starting in the low five figures for custom designs. But a few stock items are typically for sale in the display room. Browsers are warmly welcomed, and it's always fun just to watch Andy Holand tattooing a good mambo on his latest work-in-progress, or to flip through the portfolio books of his and his late partner Travis Tuck's past work. Many of their unique works adorn off-island homes and buildings, from a Steven Spielberg–commissioned velociraptor to the Nittany Lion over Penn State's Beaver Stadium. You'll also find Tuck's designs atop a couple of local town halls, supermarkets, the *Gazette* offices in Edgartown, and the hospital.

Past Tuck & Holand, State Road is the province of a strip of shops geared mostly toward errand-runners, but past the dry cleaning and home appliance center you'll also find the island's only miniature golf course, opposite Cronig's Market: **Island Cove Mini-Golf** (386 State Rd., 508/693-2611).

When all your window-shopping and art-critiquing requires more substantial sustenance than ice cream from **Mad Martha's** on Union Street, or butter-smooth fudge from **Murdick's,** at the corner of Union and Main Street, try a sandwich from **M.V. Bagel Authority** (96 Main St., 508/693-4152), or dig into a hefty turkey sandwich from **Bob's Pizza** (22 Main St., 508/693-8266), or nosh on a panini from **Beetlebung Coffee House** (32 Beach St., 508/6936-7122) between the Chamber of Commerce Visitor Center and Five Corners.

RECREATION
Beaches
Vineyard Haven has five public beaches, three of which are within a mile of downtown. Tiny **Owen Park Beach** is only a block from the Steamship Authority (SSA) dock, but it gets more use as a boat launch than as a serene spot for catching rays. Since the breakwater keeps the surf away, it's probably best appreciated by really small kids—but if you have some time to kill before catching the ferry, it's good for soaking tired feet. The area to the left of the wooden town pier is private, by the way. From the SSA, either cut through the parking lot behind the bank, or step up to Main and follow the one-way traffic one block to the bandstand; that's Owen Park. The beach is at the bottom of the hill.

Farther up Main Street, about three-quarters of a mile from the cinema, is the **Tisbury Town Beach** (also called Bayside), an 80-foot sliver of sandy harbor shoreline between stone jetties at the end of Owen Little Way, from which you can watch the comings and goings at the Vineyard Haven Yacht Club next door. Free swimming lessons are given here in summer. On the other side of the harbor, about three-quarters of a mile along Beach Road toward Oak Bluffs, is **Lagoon Bridge Park,** on Lagoon Pond. Here, too, sunbathers are outnumbered, this time by water-skiers and windsurfers. (It's also the only one out of the town's four beach parks without any parking.)

Vineyard Haven's most attractive swimming beaches are about two miles from downtown near the west end of Lake Tashmoo. Facing Woods Hole and the Elizabeth Islands across Vineyard Sound (that's big Naushon stretching away to the left and tiny Nonamesset almost opposite), the ocean portion of **Wilfrid's Pond Preserve** is exemplary of the north shore: little to no surf, light winds (if any), no audible motorized boats, and water that stays relatively warm and shallow for some distance from shore. It's also quite small, which is why parking (free) is limited to space for five cars. Wilfrid's Pond itself is not open to swimmers, but the bench overlooking its brackish waters is a fine spot to forget worldly cares.

Another half mile past Wilfrid's, at the end of the same heavily gullied and potholed lane, is **Tashmoo Beach** or Herring Creek Beach (also with free parking). At first glance, it's disappointingly small, but walk back along the sandy lakeshore and you'll find the part favored by regulars. To reach either beach, make a right at the end of Daggett Avenue on the better-maintained of the two sandy tracks there by the fire hydrant.

Water Sports

The island's best all-around source for buying or renting sailboards, sea kayaks, canoes, surf- and bodyboards, and just about anything else that can skim across water under power of wind, wave, or paddle is **Wind's Up!** (199 Beach Rd., 508/693-4252, www.windsupmv.com, 9 A.M.–6 P.M. daily late-June–Aug., 10 A.M.–5:30 P.M. daily mid-June and Sept. and Tues.–Sat. Apr. and Oct., hours vary Nov.–Mar.) past the big gas tanks on Vineyard Haven's harbor. The friendly folks at this we've-got-everything emporium at Lagoon Harbor Park also offer lessons for nearly all the equipment they stock, provide car racks if you want to try the waters in another town, and for $50 will deliver to anywhere on the Vineyard for stuff you rent by the week. Sailboard rentals range from $29 an hour to $195 a week (more for expert-level boards). A small-group introductory windsurfing lesson is $60, while a full eight-hour "certification" course—two days of coaching plus three additional practice hours scheduled at your leisure—runs $110. Sea kayaks rent for $16 per hour to $150 per week (slightly more for tandem and expedition models); lessons are $50 per hour. Canoe rentals run $25 per hour to $195 per week. Half-day (4 hours), full day (24 hours), and three-day rentals are available for most items. Lifejackets are included in the rental prices—and so are wet suits, for windsurfing lessons and hourly rentals (they can be rented separately, too).

Surfers—including kitesurfers—should also check out **Corner 5 Surf** (5 Water St., 508/693-

VINEYARD BEACH BASICS

When it comes to beaches, the Vineyard has a little something for just about everybody, from bodysurfers to wading toddlers. Most, but not all, of the island's more than two dozen beaches are free and open to the public. Several on private conservation land charge seasonal access fees, and five town-owned beaches are restricted in summer to local residents and specific guests. Parking is not a given – some places have little or none, and some charge up to $20 for the privilege.

There's no nude beach per se, although discreet naturists are tolerated in select areas. Private ownership extends down to the low-water line, though, so please respect beach fences, No Trespassing signs, and community standards for shedding your Speedo.

As a rule, the strongest surf is found along the Atlantic-facing south shore, since there's no land between here and Hispaniola to dampen the ocean swells. These beaches are the first to close during foul summer weather, when prevailing southwesterly winds propel huge waves up the shore. In their wake are new underwater sandbars that build the kind of tall breakers beloved by serious boogie boarders, but hazardous to windsurfers and their equipment. Parents and timid swimmers should also be mindful of this shore's strong undertow.

Until the onslaught of winter northeasters, the east shore (facing Nantucket Sound) and the north shore (facing the Vineyard Sound) are milder. As a rule, they're also warmer. North shore beaches are reputed to have the clearest water and definitely feature the best sunsets.

3676, www.cornerfive.com, 9 A.M.–5 P.M. daily late May–early Oct., 9 A.M.–9 P.M. daily July–Aug., off-season hours by appointment), right at Five Corners next to the Black Dog Bakery. Whatever your gear needs, from board shorts to board wax, you can find it here or they'll be happy to special order it. Surfboard rentals are also available by the half or full day ($20–25).

Lagoon Pond is one of the best spots on the island for beginning and intermediate windsurfers. It's great for kayakers, too. Good winds and safety from big ships make it a two-mile-long playpen—although it sometimes buzzes with water-skiers. Access is from the adjacent public beaches. If you brought your own rig to the island by car, Sailing Park Camp in Oak Bluffs is the only Lagoon Pond public access with parking.

Sailing

Local waters are a day-sailor's delight. If you've left your yacht in San Diego, you can rent or charter something here, from a little Sunfish to a big sloop—or catch a scheduled cruise with one of several operators.

The most visible cruising outfit is undoubtedly Coastwise Packet Company, a.k.a. **Black Dog Tall Ships** (Beach St. Ext., 508/693-1699, www.theblackdogtallships.com), owned by Captain Robert Douglas, founder of the Black Dog Tavern and its spinoff merchandising empire. Coastwise has three windjammers dedicated in whole or part to daytrips ($60) and charters from mid-May through mid-October, with all three in peak service June–August.

The company flagship is the square topsail schooner, *Shenandoah,* a 152-foot (sparred length) motorless wooden ship built in 1964 specifically for passenger service. Only slightly smaller is the meticulously restored gaff-rigged pilot schooner, the *Alabama,* originally built in Pensacola in 1926. The latest addition to the fleet is the *Chantey,* an intimate 38-foot gaff-rigged schooner built in 1927 to a design by William Atkin, whose boats are highly regarded for their seaworthiness.

Both of the bigger ships dedicate several weeks in the height of summer to six-day hands-on cruises for youngsters between the ages of 9 and 16 ($850), so in July and August the only opportunity for adults to catch a sched-

windsurfing on Vineyard Haven Harbor

uled cruise on the *Shenandoah* or *Alabama* may be on Saturday. Fortunately each has room for dozens of passengers, so it's rare to be turned away even on the day of sailing, although reservations are strongly encouraged.

Day sails on the big vessels last three hours, and of course go wherever the wind blows. You'll be able to lend a hand in raising the thousands of square feet of sail, if you wish, and can share the wheel with the captain, too. Or simply enjoy the salt-sea breeze, the slap of waves on the hull, the hum of the wind through the rigging, and the curious gulls overhead while enjoying a complimentary glass of wine. Trips aboard the *Chantey,* which takes a maximum of only six passengers, are two hours (1–3 P.M. and 5–7 P.M. June–Aug). For reservations or information on the fleet's current sailing schedule, drop by the office at the foot of the wharf beside the Black Dog Tavern.

A variety of other options exist for leisure sailing out of Vineyard Haven Harbor during the summer. You could, for instance, call and see if there's a space aboard the

HIKES AND RAMBLES

Nearly a thousand Vineyard acres are available for your recreational use, mostly in the form of small preserves with simple trail systems winding through fields and forests, around ponds and wetlands, and along shorelines and streambeds. All but a handful are free, and nearly all are open dawn to dusk year-round, except during deer hunting week (beginning after Thanksgiving). An excellent, free, island-wide map identifying all accessible conservation properties is available by mail from the **Martha's Vineyard Land Bank Commission** (P.O. Box 2057, Edgartown 02539), or you can pick up a copy in person from their office in Edgartown (167 Main St., 508/627-7141, www.mvlandbank.com).

Trail maps to individual properties are usually posted at the trailheads nearest car and bike parking; if no map is present, the trail is most likely a straightforward loop or something equally self-evident. For the ultimate peace of mind, pick up a copy of Will Flender's thorough *Walking Trails of Martha's Vineyard* in local bookstores or directly from the **Vineyard Conservation Society** (VCS), an advocacy group headquartered at the Mary Wakeman Conservation Center off Lambert's Cove Road in Vineyard Haven (18 Helen Ave., 508/693-9588, www.vcsmv.org).

Two other land-saving organizations – the Sheriff's Meadow Foundation and Vineyard Open Land Foundation – share office space with the VCS at the Wakeman Center; besides selling Flender's book and dispensing free information about their individual missions, the center hosts workshops and fundraisers and is the starting point for anyone interested in hiking around the adjacent 22 acres of ponds and cranberry bogs.

In addition to guided programs held in season at the selected properties included here, both the VCS and the Land Bank conduct off-season monthly walks on island conservation land. The VCS series (every second Sunday, Oct.-Mar.) typically includes at least one hike on privately owned, undeveloped land not otherwise open to the public; the last event of the season is an island-wide beach cleanup on Earth Day in April. The Land Bank series (every first Sunday, Nov.-May) showcases the organization's own fine properties until their culminating full-day cross-island hike on National Trails Day, the first Saturday in June. Both island weeklies, the *Vineyard Gazette* and the *Martha's Vineyard Times,* announce starting times and meeting places a few days before each walk, or you can get the skinny straight from the friendly staff at either organization. When choosing your apparel, by the way, remember that these hikes are often wet or muddy.

The Trustees of Reservations (508/693-7392, www.thetrustees.org), which preserves several of the most noteworthy island properties through both outright ownership and conservation restrictions (CRs) held on otherwise still-private land, offers off-season hikes and walks, too, although usually for Trustees members only. Led by the staff naturalist, such "CR walks" give members a peek at not-yet-public parcels like "the Brickyard" and Squibnocket Point. Instructions for becoming a Trustees member ($45 for individuals, $65 for families) can be found on their website.

Final notes: While some conservation properties ban mountain biking on their trails, the State Forest allows it, and in many cases, so does the Land Bank. You'll find each property's policy about bikes – and pets, too – at bulletin boards near the trailhead parking areas. And anyone interested in gathering live shellfish at any of the pond or bayside properties must obtain a town license from the shellfish warden at the appropriate town hall.

Ena (508/627-0848, www.sailena.com, $60 per person for three hours), a 34-foot John Alden–designed wooden sloop. Or consider the **Liberty** (508/560-2464, www.sloop liberty.com, $55 per person for three hours), a 40-foot gaff-rigged sloop built by the Vineyard's very own specialists in wooden boat construction, Gannon & Benjamin. Both are also available for full-day private sailing trips in local waters.

If you want more than just a little half-day cruise on which someone else plays skipper while you feel the wind and spray, you're looking for a term charter. ("Bareboat charters," the arrangement whereby you flash your skipper's license and sign a lot of expensive pieces of paper and walk away with a big boat at your command for a week, aren't available on the Vineyard.) One of the more notable charter opportunities available in July and August is aboard the 64-foot Alden-designed schooner, **When and If** (201/739-8810, www.schooner whenandif.com), built for General George Patton in 1939. Whether you want to sail by for a few days or a few weeks, New Jersey–based Ruitenberg Charters provides the captain, crew, cook, and all housekeeping gear; you simply provide the passengers (up to 15) and your own beach towels.

Would you prefer solo sailing—or beginners' lessons on something you can haul out of the water without a crane? **Wind's Up!** (119 Beach Rd., 508/693-4252, www.windsupmv .com) rents Sunfish and similar-sized boats for $35 per hour, $110 per day; or slightly larger catamarans for $40 per hour, $125 per day. Instruction runs $90 or $100 per hour for two or three learners, or splurge on five private lessons for $320.

ACCOMMODATIONS
Under $50
The Vineyard's best budget option for overnight stays is camping. Since the island doesn't offer much of a backcountry wilderness experience, fiscal austerity is about the only reason to camp. The only place to do it is **Martha's Vineyard Family Campground** (Edgartown Rd., 508/693-3772, www.campmvfc.com, late May–mid-October). It mostly attracts RV-style campers, but tenters are tolerated. Rates start at $48 for tent sites for two adults, $4 per child, or $54 for a trailer or RV and two adults. They rent pop-up campers, too. No dogs or motorcycles are permitted.

$100-150
In summer, the pickings in this price range can be counted on your thumbs. One is the **Kinsman House** (278 Main St., 508/693-2311, $125 d), built in 1880 as the rectory of a local church. Located at the corner of Tashmoo Street, on the quiet end of Main where big homes sit behind stone walls and large lawns. The three rooms here provide simple comfort with shared bath and no breakfast (one room actually has an en suite toilet, but must still share the shower). The proprietor, Doreen—only the property's third owner—keeps her prices low partly as a deliberate act of resistance against the economics of exclusion that have turned the Vineyard into a playground for the super wealthy (she herself is a school teacher).

Built back when President Jefferson was welcoming Lewis and Clark home from their river trip, **The Look Inn** (13 Look St., 508/693-6893, year-round, $125 d), at the corner of William Street, offers a casual antidote to the stereotypical B&B's dust-ruffled, four-poster decor. "No bows" vow hosts Catherine and Freddy of their restored farmhouse. Their aesthetic leans instead toward futons and contemporary prints in tasteful, chintz-free rooms with sinks tucked in corners to make sharing the bath that much easier. The serenity of the breakfast table beside the garden's little ornamental fish pool will make Main Street's bustle seem much farther away than the few blocks it really is—which is only fitting for the home of a yoga teacher and massage therapist.

Outside of high season, many of the pricier larger inns—including nearly all those cited in the higher price categories to follow—offer something in this range until at least mid-May and again after late October.

ADVICE ABOUT ACCOMMODATIONS

Any skeptic who doubts the Vineyard's hotspot reputation obviously hasn't tried to book a room here in summer, when the island's 100-plus inns, B&Bs, motels, hotels, guesthouses, and resorts are as full as Las Vegas on a Saturday night. Demand is strong enough to keep many innkeepers busy playing their annual game of brinkmanship with visitors, ratcheting up room rates and lengthening minimum-stay requirements until customers cry uncle. So far, most visitors aren't blinking, so scores of the island's rooms now easily top $200, and few accept single-night bookings (not only in high season, but also on weekends and holidays most of the year).

If these stats make you blink, don't give up hope – just modify your expectations. Staying flexible with your travel dates, sharing a bathroom, accepting smaller quarters, and settling for rooms without views are all tactics for maximizing your chance of locating lodging. Leaving junior at home may help, too, since most B&Bs and small inns cultivate a kid-free atmosphere. As a rule, the fewer antiques or the larger the establishment, the more likely it welcomes families.

Speaking of expectations, traditional B&B lovers should be warned that full breakfasts are possibly the island's rarest amenity. If waking up to eggs Benedict, fresh fruit pancakes, or crêpes is why you're choosing a B&B, inquire carefully about what's for breakfast *before* guaranteeing that three-night reservation with the nonrefundable deposit.

Looking for a place with a private beach? You can count the number of candidates on your hands. Most of the beaches are like small sandboxes on busy boat-filled harbors anyway. As an alternative, consider up-island accommodations that afford guests the privilege of visiting large, beautiful, town beaches restricted to local residents – or try for one of the many rooms across the street from Oak Bluffs' or Katama's broad public beaches.

Off-season's popular object of desire – the bedroom warmed by a nice crackling winter fire – is likewise available at just a dozen or so properties, although a score more have hearths in living rooms or other common areas. Can you sit by the fire and watch Neptune hurl waves against the shore outside? Only from a distance. This island is made of sand, not stone; outside of the tranquil confines of Vineyard Haven's inner harbor, any lodging built that close to any coastline not reinforced by concrete would wash away in a year. Private fireplaces and full breakfasts? Again, mostly no, but there is one notable exception – the Jonathan Munroe House in Edgartown.

$150-250

The vast majority of the Vineyard's lodging choices are small inns and adult-oriented B&Bs. If you're a family of four or just prefer free HBO to small talk over breakfast with strangers, make a beeline for the **Vineyard Harbor Motel** (60 Beach Rd., 508/693-3334, www.vineyardharbormotel.com, $150–190 d). It's one of the few properties on the island with its own private beach, a short stretch of sand fronting the boat-filled harbor. Some rooms come with a full kitchen, too, including the penthouse king-bedded suite, which is a comparative bargain at $210.

A contemporary bed and breakfast with distinctive character, **Marni's House** (122 Holly Tree Ln., 508/696-6198, www.marnishouse.com, May–Oct., $175–220 d) sits in tranquility at the edge of the West Chop woods, some 80 acres of conservation land frequented by deer and birds. A 20-minute walk along Old Lighthouse Road, a now-disused ancient way through the trees, brings you right to the heart of town. The trio of modern rooms are each quite different from one another (one even has an enameled Japanese *ofuro*, a barrel-shaped soaking tub), but all have outdoor wooden decks among the trees, and of course guests share in the bountiful homemade breakfasts, including Marni's daily handmade breads.

COURTESY OF THE MASION HOUSE

a king suite at the Mansion House

At the corner of State Road and Edgartown Road about 10 minutes' walk from downtown is the **Twin Oaks Inn** (20–28 Edgartown Rd., www.twinoaksinn.net), comprising two distinctly separate properties. The more traditional B&B of the pair is the **Clark House** (508/693-6550 or 866/493-6550, $150–235 d), whose enclosed front porch is well equipped with comfortable rocking chairs. Its five rooms, all with private baths, come in sizes suitable for families as well as couples. The other half is the adjacent **Hanover House** (508/696-6099 or 800/696-8633, $185–245 d), a perfect example of a classic New England country inn. Dating to the 1860s, this spacious property offers a dozen rooms and a trio of suites, including two with full kitchens. It coddles guests with antiques, an inviting porch, sunny decks, and an atmosphere that makes you feel right at home. A bunch of complimentary bicycles are available for Twin Oaks guests—"the early bird gets the bike"— along with beach towels, beach chairs, and even sandcastle-building tools for anyone who would like them. There is WiFi if you truly are jonesing to catch up on email from the office, and a continental homemade breakfast is included.

Some Vineyard accommodations seem to target people who would sooner empty their wallets than sit on the same porcelain as strangers. Others earn their higher rates with more than just a private commode and complimentary basket of tiny shampoo bottles. One of the more attractive values in this category is the **Greenwood House** (40 Greenwood Ave., 508/693-6150, www.greenwoodhouse.com, $199–269 d), two doors away from the public library on Main Street. The handful of rooms are all decorated with one eye toward period appearances—the house dates to 1906—and the other toward creature comforts: air-conditioning, color cable TV, mini-refrigerator, hair dryers, phones, and, of course, private baths. A full breakfast is included, too.

East of downtown is a quiet residential area occupying high ground overlooking the harbor. Here just minutes' walk from shops and restaurants sits **The Doctor's House Bed & Breakfast** (60 Mt. Aldworth Rd., 508/696-0859 or 866/507-6670, www.doctorshouse .com, $200–285 d), on two landscaped acres above wooded Cat Hollow. Built in 1906, this Arts and Crafts mansion offers over half a dozen rooms to guests seeking period decor and traditional B&B comforts, from the little welcome gift of locally-made chocolate to the full cooked-to-order breakfast.

$250 and Up

The most stylish and luxurious property in town is the (**Mansion House** (9 Main St., 508/693-2200 or 800/332-4112, www .mvmansionhouse.com, $279–319 d), right smack in the center of town. While outwardly resembling a classic clapboard "painted lady" Victorian resort, it is in fact thoroughly modern, having risen from the ashes of the 2001 fire that burned its historic predecessor to the ground. The gables, bays, verandas, balustrades, and lofty cupola are all an architectural tip of the hat to the past, but inside the decor eschews frills and lace in favor of a clean Californian sun-drenched look. New construction means no creaking 19th-century floors, wafer-thin walls, or plumbing shoehorned into former closets— instead the spacious rooms feature central air, soundproofing, and full-sized bathrooms. Some deluxe units and suites ($359–516) also come with oversized plasma TVs, gas fireplaces, and porches that look out over the harbor, and all guests can relax on the rooftop deck with its lovely panoramic views. Rates include breakfast at the inn's restaurant, and there is a full spa and health club on the premises, complete with 75- foot indoor pool and enough fitness equipment to keep up with your customary cardio or free- weight regimen.

FOOD

Easily the most famous Vineyard restau- rant is **The Black Dog Tavern** (21 Beach St. Extension, 508/693-9223, www.theblackdog .com, 7 A.M.–10 P.M. daily mid-May–Dec., 7 A.M.–3 P.M. daily and 5–close Fri.–Sun. Jan.–early May, $14–31), next to the ferry stag- ing area in Vineyard Haven, behind the Black Dog bakery-cum-clothing-store full of Black Dog brand wearables. The T-shirts have been sighted around the world, from Patagonia to Nepal, and if you're grabbing a snack at the bakery counter, you may marvel that global

fame hasn't brought about tremendous price hikes. The tavern's prices, on the other hand, are more typical of the island's best dining spots, although it isn't one of them—not for dinner, at any rate. Better to come for break- fast, when you can enjoy the harbor view and nautical mementos without breaking the bank. It's absolutely mobbed in summers; no reserva- tions accepted. While it doesn't have the full menu of the downtown location, the Black Dog's satellite Bakery Café, on State Road at the southern edge of town, nearly opposite the turnoff for the Tisbury Park & Ride, is a good alternative for up-island visitors who want to sample the muffins, chowder, or burgers but avoid the morass of Five Corners traffic.

Named after its original owners, the (**ArtCliff Diner** (39 Beach Rd., 508/693- 1224, 7 A.M.–2 P.M. daily Thurs.–Tues. year- round except April) is now presided over by a former White House pastry chef—but don't think that means the menu is all sweetness and light. *Au contraire,* you'll find hearty choices from steak 'n eggs to potato pancakes, al- though admittedly everything is done up with a Vineyard touch: fresh-squeezed OJ, fine herb and nut breads, plenty of vegetarian options to complement the burgers and lobster rolls, or- ganic yogurt with the granola, and fine Vermont cheddar for the grilled cheese. Breakfast mavens can order their favorite egg dishes right up till closing. So, what are you waiting for?

When dinnertime rolls around, most din- ers seem to head to Oak Bluffs and Edgartown, where liquor licenses are in ready supply. If you don't miss having alcohol with your eve- ning meal—or if you've come prepared, bottle- filled brown bag in hand—consider cruising the Mediterranean from the comfort of your dinner table at (**Mediterranean** (52 Beach Rd., 508/693-1617, www.med-mv.com, 6 P.M.– close Thurs.–Sat. mid-Apr.–mid-May, daily late May–mid-Oct., Thurs.–Sun. late Oct.–early Nov., $28–33), opposite Ace Hardware on the industrial side of busy Five Corners. This charming waterfront restaurant overlooks the swaying masts in the boat anchorage just outside the big picture windows and draws on the culinary traditions of countries from North Africa and Spain to the Levant. The menu artfully blends familiar local ingredients with preparations found nowhere else on the Vineyard.

If these prices leave no room for risk-taking, make a beeline for **Nicky's Italian Café** (395 State Rd., 508/696-2020, www.nickys italiancafe.com, noon–2 P.M. Mon.–Fri., 5:30 P.M.–close daily July–Aug., 5:30 P.M.–close Mon.–Sat. the rest of the year, $12–28), located behind Radio Shack in the commercial block adjacent to Cronig's Market, on the very busy stretch of State Road almost a mile from the harbor (take VTA bus 2, 3, or 10). Nicky's is a casual lunch-and-dinner spot favored by locals both for its reliable cuisine and its prices.

For the ultimate seaside vacation meal, try a bluefish sandwich and soft-serve ice cream from **Sandy's Fish & Chips** (State Rd., 508/693-1220, 11 A.M.–7 P.M. Mon.–Sat. late Apr.–Sept.), at the corner of Martin Street in the same building as John's Fish Market. While Sandy's can certainly fill your beach basket, picnickers who prefer to play Dagwood and build sandwiches from scratch are best served by the friendly **Tisbury Farm Market,** across from Cronig's Market. You'll find imported cheeses, olives, and other fixings—and high-quality baguettes, focaccia, and other fresh loaves to put 'em on.

VINEYARD DINING

Unlike Cape Cod, the Vineyard doesn't consume its weight in frying oil each day. Fish and chips are available if you want them, but most Vineyard eateries compete for either the country-club surf-and-turf set or upscale palates accustomed to fine comestibles at high prices. Local epicures have come to expect fresh herbs, organic greens, bottled water, and meat-free menu selections (if it isn't on the menu, ask). Even delis and fried-seafood shacks cater to health-conscious herbivores with veggie burgers. If you enjoy wine with your dinner, remember that Oak Bluffs and Edgartown are the only Vineyard communities where you can buy alcohol in stores or restaurants. If you're dining in one of the island's dry towns, be sure to bring your own – and expect a small corkage fee to be added to the bill.

Most places stay open seven days a week in season, then cut back days and hours when business becomes more uneven. Before or after the June-August season, confirm that your destination restaurant is open before making any pilgrimage.

Oak Bluffs

Although even the meadow voles in the most remote acre of the island must by now recognize the tremors of The Season, possibly no place is as utterly transformed by the summer crowd as Oak Bluffs. From its chaste beginnings as host to great Methodist tent revival meetings, "OB" has evolved into the most honky-tonk town on the Vineyard, thanks to its after-dark appeal to the under-25 crowd.

Blue-blooded Nantucketers, raised to see the Vineyard as a mongrel cross between Coney Island, Kmart, and a sailors' bar, get goose bumps just thinking of what goes on here, but it's no Fort Lauderdale or Virginia Beach—or

even Santa Cruz. Compared to the rest of the Vineyard, though, there's no denying that on summer evenings, this joint jumps. Cars prowl along "the Circuit" (Circuit Avenue, downtown's main drag), the small handful of nightclubs and bars pulse with music and pheromones, and even underage kids get giddy in the swirl of yearning, strolling up and down the Avenue with gossipy enthusiasm, eyeing members of the opposite sex, and lapping up lots of ice cream. Weekenders and tourists, meanwhile, shop and enjoy the carnival atmosphere. At summer's end, the instigators of all the fun vanish as quickly as they arrived, returning to school yards and campus quads and leaving the town as quiet as a banquet hall after a big wedding. Gone are the gaggles of teenagers, the guitarists gently strumming Kurt Cobain songs, the cross-legged rows of young sidewalk sitters. Gone are the lines at the two cinemas, and the crowds spilling out of the amusement arcade. Although the music still blares and the doors stay open until at least Columbus Day, more often than not it feels as if staff outnumber patrons as the end of daylight saving time rolls around. The rapid exodus of the town's spirited lifeblood makes OB the first down-island town every year to roll up its summer finery and shutter its colorful facades. Restaurants and accommodations nearly all close by the middle of October, with the pleasant exception of the least expensive eateries, several of which remain open year-round.

But OB's appeal isn't confined to the young. On the contrary, all but the most rural-minded travelers may find it to be the best base for exploring the whole Vineyard. By bus, car, or bike, it's as favorably connected to the rest of the island as you can get, and has ferry connections to more ports—including Nantucket and Rhode Island—than any other island town. Its restaurants and accommodations fit nearly all price ranges—which is more than can be said of any other place on either the Vineyard or Nantucket. It offers some of the most interesting street fairs and special events, from winter's Chili Contest to summer's Jazzfest. It has the most number of ice cream parlors, including **Carousel Ice Cream Factory** (15 Circuit Ave., 508/696-8614, 10:30 A.M.–11 P.M. daily July–early Sept., daily hours vary March–Nov.), possibly the best, and, across the street, **Ben & Bill's Chocolate Emporium** (12 Circuit Ave., 508/696-0008, 11 A.M.–midnight daily July–early Sept., daily hours vary May–mid-Oct.), possibly the most fanciful—try the lobster flavor for proof, or "moose droppings." Even the beach and brewpub are but a stroll from your most accommodations. All this is wrapped in a fanciful Victorian frame of Gothic Revival and Queen Anne architecture.

SIGHTS
Flying Horses Carousel

It doesn't take a kid or a carousel buff to appreciate the craftsmanship of the landmark **Flying Horses** (508/693-9481), a contemporary of Coney Island's first merry-go-round. The 22 colorful steeds, adorned with real horsehair, were carved in 1876 by C. W. F. Dare. (Although it claims to be the nation's oldest working carousel, Rhode Island has an 1870 contender for the title.) Rides are $1.50, and if you grab one of the brass rings at the right time, you get another ride for free. (You can tell which kids have been on-island for a while by the number of rings they're able to grab at once.) Located on Lake Avenue smack between downtown and the harbor, the carousel is open 11 A.M.–4 P.M. weekends from Easter Sunday through early May and then daily through early October; between Memorial Day and Labor Day, it stays open until 10 P.M. nightly.

◖ Oak Bluffs Campground

Just behind the commercial storefronts along Circuit Avenue lies a carpenters' jigsaw fantasia of the former Wesleyan Grove, now formally known as the M. V. Camp Meeting Association grounds, whose tent revivals begat both OB and the island's tourist industry. Stroll through the Arcade on Circuit Avenue and you'll discover a riot of colorful little cottages encircling Trinity Park and its large, open-sided Tabernacle like wagons drawn up around a campfire—hidden from downtown by design.

The tall fence and limited entry points were originally intended to restrict the secular influences of the resort community springing up right in the pious campers' backyard. The closely packed cottages—which truly deserve the name, unlike the extravagances perched upon the seaside cliffs of Newport—evoke the intimacy of the tent encampment, whose early years were dominated by big tents shared by whole congregations. The steeply pitched roofs and twin-leaf front doors are deliberate allusions to the A-frame tents and their entrance flaps.

If the Campground seems too neighborly for comfort by modern suburban standards, re-

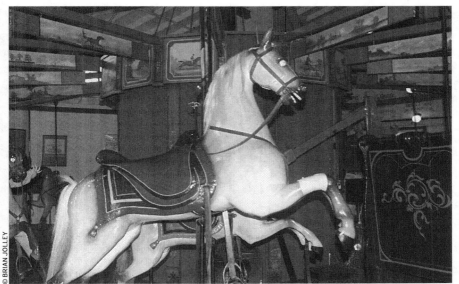

© BRIAN JOLLEY

Flying Horses Carousel is the oldest continually operating carousel in the country.

member that in the 1860s, when most of these were built, the average huge hotels in America's most popular resorts were about as communal as you could get, with just about every waking hour spent in the company of fellow guests. For these happy campers, the mutual lives and close ties to their neighbors were not only customary, they were a source of their security. The ethos of the private car and private bath was still over half a century away when most of these little houses were built, and it shows.

With the exception of the 1879 wrought-iron and sheet-metal Tabernacle, the Campground is a celebration of the power woodworking tools newly available in the latter half of the 19th century. The gingerbread, porch railings, and window shutters are a catalog of imagination, from the decorative (arabesques and French curves) to the narrative (a hunter and hound chasing a hare). Stop by the **Cottage Museum** (1 Trinity Park, 508/693-0525, www.mvcma.org, 10 A.M.–4 P.M. Mon.–Sat. and 1–4 P.M. Sun. mid-June–mid-Oct., $2) for some free advice on locating the architectural highlights. Pony up the nominal admission fee and you can also check out the mu-

seum's collection of furnishings—typical of the Campground's Victorian heyday. Some nights in summer, the Tabernacle is used for musical performances, from Wednesday evening community sings to weekend concerts; if you're visiting in August, check the events listings in the local papers for information.

One of the early secular alternatives to gospel preaching was **Illumination Night,** begun by the Oak Bluffs Company in 1869. Houses in both that company's resort development, outside Wesleyan Grove, and the Methodist Campground itself were bedecked with Japanese lanterns and banners that humorously commingled the sacred and the profane in such messages as, "We Trust in Providence, Rhode Island." Now, on the third Wednesday each August, Trinity Park and the surrounding cottages perpetuate the lantern-hanging tradition as part of a community event sponsored by the Camp Meeting Association.

Ocean Park

Fronting Nantucket Sound, surrounded by the turrets and balconies of OB's most spacious

STRAWBERRY FIELDS FOREVER

One of the increasingly rare chunks of down-island open land that hasn't been turned into house lots, **Whippoorwill Farm** (80 Stoney Hill Rd., 508/693-5995) deserves special mention because it's the only place on the island where you can pick a basket of succulent strawberries.

Strawberries are usually ready for picking around the second week of June and continue at least until the end of the month; depending on the timing of their crops, some plants bear fruit throughout July as well. Call ahead to check on the pickings.

Straddling three townships — West Tisbury, Tisbury, and Oak Bluffs — Whippoorwill Farm is most easily reached from the OB side. Take the signposted turn off the Edgartown-Vineyard Haven Road (about a 0.25 mile northwest of Barnes Road) and follow Stoney Hill Road another 0.5 mile west. Don't pay attention to the Private sign at the gates of the fancy Iron Hill Farm housing development, by the way — maybe it helps to justify adding another digit to the value of those pondside estates, or is a minuscule deterrent to the moped-riding six-pack-toting teens who used to hang out here, but the road is most assuredly public.

mansions, seven-acre Ocean Park is the focal point of many festivities. An ornate bandstand, built in anticipation of President Grant's 1874 visit, sits on the huge lawn like a fancy stickpin on a bolt of green felt; here in July and August, **free concerts** by the Vineyard Band are held on alternate Sunday evenings. Here, too, are the best seats in the house for August's end-of-season **fireworks display,** which doubles as a fundraiser for the local fire department. Other times in summer, it harbors basking couples, Frisbee players, and small kids running themselves silly. Admirers of **Victorian architecture** can stroll the park boundary and find a textbook of picturesque styles: hints of a Tuscan villa here and a Swiss chalet there, Queen Anne towers and piazzas, Craftsman- and Shingle-style influences, and the ubiquitous fancy roof and porch trim deriving from the town specialty—carpenter gothic.

In the small portion of the park near the police station stands a monument to the end of the Civil War—"The Chasm is closed," begins its inscription. Though it definitely depicts a bronze Union soldier (notice the "U.S." on his belt buckle), the local resident who bestowed the statue as a gift to the town was also a veteran of the 21st Regiment of Virginia, which is why there's a tablet dedicated "in honor of the Confederate soldiers" on the pedestal.

East Chop Light

At the suburban tip of East Chop along East Chop Drive sits the East Chop Light, originally the island's only private lighthouse. In 1869, Captain Silas Daggett ventured his own money to build the navigational aid, then solicited contributions for its support from fellow captains, ship owners, and marine insurance companies. Besides alleged difficulty collecting after vessels had arrived safely, the civic-minded captain's first tower also burned down and had to be replaced—at no small expense. Eventually, the U.S. government bought the whole thing off Daggett. Finding his lantern building to be "little better than a shanty," the Federal Lighthouse Board approved construction of the cast-iron present structure in 1878. The name on the sign, Telegraph Hill, predates the light by a generation. In the early 19th century, a semaphore tower occupied the spot and sent shipping news from the island to Woods Hole for relay to owners and underwriters in Boston. In the middle of the century, that tower was replaced by an underwater telegraph cable.

Now leased from the Coast Guard by the local historical society (508/627-4441, www.marthasvineyardhistory.org), the light is open to the public for sunset viewing on summer Friday evenings late June through early

October, from 90 minutes prior to sundown to 30 minutes after; admission is $3.

ENTERTAINMENT

A frequent contributor to summertime cultural performances is Oak Bluffs' octagonal **Union Chapel** (508/693-5350) on the upper end of Circuit Avenue. Free organ recitals fill the warmly resonant wooden interior on summer Wednesdays at noon, while a variety of other musical offerings—from Shaker songs to piano jazz—fills up many an evening between the end of June and the end of August.

Clubs and Pubs

With one significant exception in Edgartown, nearly all the nightclub action on the island occurs on Circuit Avenue in Oak Bluffs. Case in point: stand at the foot of Circuit Avenue and you can have your pick of **The Lampost,** which also contains **The Dive Bar** in the basement and **Sinners & Saints** on the second floor (6 Circuit Ave., 508/693-4032, www.lampostmv.com, 4 P.M.–12:30 A.M. Mon.–Fri., 12:30 P.M.–12:30 A.M. Sat.–Sun., closed in the off-season); **The Ritz Café** (4 Circuit Ave., 508/693-9851, 4 A.M.–midnight daily); and **Seasons** (19 Circuit Ave., 508/693-7129, www.seasonspub.com, 5:30 P.M.–close daily). All are bars that do their utmost to uphold lower Circuit Avenue's reputation as a party street, sometimes against a background of live music by local bands, but more often against ESPN, jukeboxes, and loud conversation fueled by cheap drinks.

For more of a piano-bar atmosphere—albeit an occasionally rockin' piano bar—check out the lounge at **The Island House** (11 Circuit Ave., 508/693-4516, www.islandhousemv.com, 5 P.M.–close June–Sept., call for off-season hours), opposite The Lampost. **Offshore Ale House** (30 Kennebec Ave., 508/693-2626, www.offshoreale.com) has Irish *sessiuns* and other live acoustic performances. After the summer crowds abate, Seasons trades some of its dining tables for pool tables; the Lampost and its associated club rooms close down completely.

While several island restaurants are known for their musical offerings, **Lola's** (15 Island Inn Rd., 508/693-5007, www.lolassouthernseafood.com, 5 P.M.–close daily), the Southern-styled restaurant at the Island Inn off Beach Road on the southern outskirts of OB, is the king of the lot. Its pub offers plenty of live blues, roots, funk, R&B, and jazz year-round (nightly July–Aug., at least weekends otherwise). In July and August there's live tunes during Sunday brunch, too—including, a couple times each summer, rousing spirit-raising soul-saving Gospel music.

Note that island-wide ordinances ban smoking in all restaurants *and* bars.

SHOPPING

Anyone disembarking from the ferries at Oak Bluffs Harbor will be forgiven for initially thinking that T-shirt, postcard, and candy shops are the only retail trade on offer in downtown OB. In spite of the fact that some of the stores contain the word "gallery" in their names, the only art in the Dockside Market Place by the Hy-Line pier is strictly of the tourist variety. Away from the harbor, past the bars and cafés, the main drag becomes slightly more recognizably part of a real town, with diner-like lunch counters and general merchandisers holding back-to-school sales in the fall.

Amid all the shops competing for your attention, it isn't hard to pick out the vivid and whimsical window display at **Craftworks** (42 Circuit Ave., 508/693-7463, www.craftworksgallery.com, 11 A.M.–5 P.M. daily Mar.–May, 10 A.M.–9 P.M. daily June–Aug., 10 A.M.–5 P.M. daily Sept.–Dec. and Sat.–Sun. Jan.–Feb.). From bold Marisol-style folk art to the kind of pottery Keith Haring might have kept around his loft, even their functional crafts exude fun.

If brass temple bells, Peruvian woolens, or things made of kinte cloth are more your style, check out the **Third World Trading Company** (52 Circuit Ave., 508/693-5550, www.thirdworldtrading.com, 10 A.M.–10 P.M. daily June–Aug., daily hours vary Sept.–early Nov. and Apr.–May, noon–4 P.M. Thurs.–Mon.

mid-Nov.–Mar.), a few doors up the block. There's apparel at **Cousen Rose Gallery** (71 Upper Circuit Ave., 508/693-6656, www.cousen rose.com, 5–9 P.M. Fri. and 11 A.M.–5 P.M. Sat.–Sun. Memorial Day–June, 10 A.M.–9 P.M. Mon.–Sat. and 11 A.M.–5 P.M. Sun. July–Labor Day, daily hours vary through mid-Sept.), past the pottery store at the top of the avenue, but it earns its name with its range of monoprints, pastels, watercolors, and other small painterly work. Don't miss the collection of children's books, either.

Arts District

Located about a quarter mile from the harbor on Dukes County Avenue, around the corner of Vineyard Avenue, the Arts District comprises a small cluster of artsy businesses, from interior designers to a recording studio. A good first stop is the **Allison Shaw Gallery** (88 Dukes County Ave., 508/696-7429, www.allisonshaw .com, by chance or appointment year-round), in a renovated wood-shingled fire station painted a dusky cerulean blue. Inside you'll find posters, notecards, and fine-art giclée prints of the owner's striking photography, along with Vineyard-themed books she has illustrated, from coffeetable volumes of sumptuous color to cookbooks celebrating local products.

The adjacent **Periwinkle Studio** (92 Dukes County Ave., 508/696-8304, by chance or appointment year-round) is a working artist's space that periodically also turns itself into a gallery for solo or group shows. Across the street is the **Dragonfly Gallery** (91 Dukes County Ave., 508/693-8877, www.mvdragon fly.com, noon–6 P.M. Thurs.–Sun. May–mid-Oct. plus Wed. July–Aug.), whose exhibitions of contemporary fine art usually reflect more ethnic and international diversity than is usual in this business. Sharing the other half of the same building is a cozy little boutique, **Red Mannequin** (93 Dukes County Ave., 508/693-2858, noon–7 P.M. Wed.–Mon. mid-June–early Sept., noon–5 P.M. Fri.–Sat. and varied other days mid-Sept.–mid-Oct. and Apr.–early June, closed mid-Oct.–Mar.), featuring fashions and jewelry with a funky SoHo-style flair.

Judy, the proprietor, favors designers a little out of couture's mainstream—from the UK and Boston, for instance—whose lightweight knits and washable silks prove that dressing up need never be dull.

The Arts District ends with Isabella Stewart Gardner eclecticism at **Pik-Nik** (99 Dukes County Ave., 508/693-1366, www.piknikmv .com, daily by chance or appointment late May–early Oct., and by chance or appointment the rest of the year, too), in the large clapboard home of professional fashion stylist Michael Hunter. Clothing for men and women, from edgy European designers such as Vivienne Westwood, doyenne of punk and darling of Mayfair couture, to shoes from Timberland UK, is juxtaposed with home goods—think modern Bauer stoneware, as bright and festive as the classic collectible originals; radical porcelain forms by the Czech design shop Qubus; and re-interpretations of iconic English china patterns by Wedgwood artist Robert Dawson. Toss in contemporary and abstract paintings and sculpture and you have a mashup of art and apparel unlike anything else on the Vineyard. A highly selective collection of vintage housewares occupies the breezeway behind the house, while the barn in back is where you'll find rotating art shows with an Island focus.

Thirsty shoppers and cyclists will find plenty of refreshment in the coolers at **Tony's Market** (119 Dukes County Ave., 508/693-4799), just down the street. Tony's has good pizzas and huge double-stuffed deli subs, too.

RECREATION
Beaches

Running discontinuously below Seaview Avenue's sidewalk promenade is the **OB Town Beach,** the most central of OB's four. Except when low tides expose a decent swath of sand, it's narrow and often gravelly—especially at the northern end, between the harbor entrance and the ferry pier at Ocean Park. Near the foot of huge, grassy Waban Park is the most pleasant and popular part, nicknamed the Inkwell, with lifeguards and swimming lessons in summer. South of the Inkwell, the **Joseph A. Sylvia**

State Beach stretches in a broad two-mile crescent between OB and Edgartown (which calls its end **Bend-in-the-Road Beach**). Backed by the windsurfing haven of Sengekontacket Pond, facing the gentle kid-friendly waves of Cow Bay, and easily accessible by the paved OB-Edgartown bike path, State Beach is deservedly one of the island's most popular.

Facing Vineyard Haven Harbor is calm, clear little **Eastville Beach** (minimal parking) beside the Lagoon drawbridge and riprap-lined channel underneath. Although lacking the sheer beachcombing breadth of State Beach, it's a good dipping spot for cyclists or neighboring cottage renters, and a prized spot for sunset views. The handkerchief-sized beach at **Sailing Camp Park** (a former Lagoon Pond Girl Scout camp off Barnes Road in the wooded residential edge of town), is only recommendable as a put-in for windsurfers—despite the diving raft offshore.

Kayaking

Try your hand at paddling around in local inshore waters with **Island Spirit Sea-Kayak Adventures** (508/693-9727, www.islands spirit.com). Choose from half- or full-day outings, in ponds or the ocean, under the midday sun or the full moon. Everything is provided: quality boats, dry bags for your gear, safety instruction…all you need do, basically, is show up willing to work out, perhaps get a little wet, and have some fun.

Parasailing and Power Boating

Got an itch to sail *over* water? Consider parasailing with **Martha's Vineyard Ocean Sports** (Dockside Marina, Oak Bluffs, 508/693-8476, www.mvoceansports.com, daily late May–mid-Oct., $110). It's a cinch: you're rigged up on a platform on the back of a turbo-powered boat and towed up 400 feet or more in the air for a good 15-minute ride. Since dips in the water upon returning to earth are entirely optional, you can bring your camcorder without fear of submerging it and give the folks back home a satellite view of New England, including the Newport Bay Bridge in Rhode Island on the western horizon, 25 miles away.

© JEFF PERK

kite-surfing in Oak Bluffs

If you'd rather stay on the water's surface, MV Ocean Sports can take care of that, too, with water-skiing, Jet Skiing, kneeboarding, Bump & Ride inner tubes…you name it, starting at $135 for the first hour. Guided two-hour sightseeing Jet-Ski rides to Chappaquiddick are available starting at $200 for one person. Alternatively, outboard-equipped six-seat Boston Whalers may be rented for $125 per hour, $325 per half day, or $550 per eight-hour day, not including fuel.

ACCOMMODATIONS
$100-150

At first blush, Oak Bluffs visitors are among the island's most fortunate, since a handful of the town's accommodations squeak in under $150. What do these lucky super-savers get for their money? B&Bs and guesthouses with shared bathrooms; usually fans in place of air-conditioning; and fewer frilly fabrics, antique furnishings, and soundly insulated walls than typically found at higher prices.

One of the most central of all the town's

available lodgings is also one of its least expensive: the **Nashua House** (30 Kennebec Ave., 508/693-0043 or 888/343-0043, www.nashuahouse.com, $99–159 d), at Healy Way across from the Offshore Ale Company. Shared baths and simple, clean, cozy rooms with the painted wood-slat walls so typical of Oak Bluffs' lodgings are the order of the day, with AC in summer. Six of the 16 rooms have an ocean view—the beach is just 150 yards away across Ocean Park—while others share a pleasant second-floor balcony looking out over the small plaza in front of the post office.

The side streets off Seaview Avenue, near the town beach and Edgartown bike path, are lined with modest gingerbread cottages, including a number of lodgings. **Titticut Follies** (37 Narragansett Ave., 508/693-4986, www.titticutfollies.com, May–mid-Oct., $115–125 d) is a prime example: no TVs, phones, or AC here, just simple wood-floor quarters painted cheery colors a few hundred yards from the beach. A couple rooms share a cedar shower house outside. If you have an appreciation—or nostalgia—for the early postwar decades, you may especially enjoy Titticut's trundle-bed, partial-bath apartment units ($145–160 per night, $650–700 per week), whose kitchens wouldn't look out of place on *Leave It to Beaver*.

The next step up over the bare-bones guesthouse is one of the neighborhood's rustic B&Bs. Consider, for instance, **The Narragansett House** (46 Narragansett Ave., 508/693-3627 or 888/693-3627, www.narragansetthouse.com, mid-May–mid-Oct., $125–185 d), a block and a half from Circuit Avenue. Built as a hotel in the 1870s, the main building offers 13 rooms decorated in summery pastels and painted white wicker, most with a single queen bed, all with private baths and AC. The most popular rooms have private little porches from which you can sit and watch the world go by, but the wraparound front porch also has plenty of comfy rocking chairs to coax you into practicing the art of enjoying the moment. The family-reunion atmosphere engendered by reg-ular patrons is quite fitting for such a casual throwback to a pre–Holiday Inn era.

$150-250

The name of **Brady's NE SW Bed & Breakfast** (10 Canonicus Ave., 508/693-9137 or 888/693-9137, $137–157 d shared bath, $195 d private bath) reflects the blend of New England's seaside cottage-style, white wood-slat walls and the owner's penchant for Southwestern poster art. This porch-wrapped Victorian just steps from the beach has private verandas, shared baths for three of its four rooms, fans rather than AC, and a warm welcome. Traveling with your pet? Brady also welcomes dogs.

In Oak Bluffs, proximity to the beach comes at a premium price. That means if you have more on your agenda than just basking by the water's edge below the town's seawall, you can get more for your dollar by choosing lodgings on the inland side of downtown. In some cases, much more: the **❰ Admiral Benbow Inn** (81 New York Ave., 508/693-6825, www.admiral-benbow-inn.com, $165–215 d), about 15 minutes' walk from the harbor, is a beautiful Victorian B&B with seven graciously appointed rooms, all with private bath. The decor favors the clean aesthetic of light, soothing colors and simple Eastlake-style furnishings rather than chintz and cabbage roses, underscoring just how modern 19th century taste could be. The VTA bus route between Vineyard Haven, Oak Bluffs, and Edgartown passes right in front of the inn. Guests needing a respite from island exploration will find the parlor and gardens to be inviting places to relax over a book or conversation. The hospitality of the owners, Bill and Mary, will have you planning your return before your stay is over.

Several inns are smack in the center of town. In my opinion the most attractive is the **Madison Inn** (18 Kennebec Ave., 508/693-2760 or 800/564-2760, www.madisoninnmv.com, May–Oct., $179–269 d), which is as centrally located as you could ask for, being surrounded by restaurants and but a block from the Flying Horses carousel and Ocean Park. Half the rooms have two double beds, perfect for families. Clever construction and carefully selected furnishings, such as flat-panel TVs, maximize the available space, and a warm Southwestern palette gives this place a comfortable atmosphere. Peak rates are mid-June–August.

Facing the Hy-Line ferry landing at the edge of the harbor, **The Dockside Inn** (9 Circuit Ave. Ext., 508/693-2966 or 800/245-5979, www.vineyardinns.com, Apr.–Oct., $200–250 d) tips its hat to the Victorian beach resorts of a century ago and the colorful Carpenter's Gothic cottages all around town. Wide, wrap-around verandas, detailed woodwork, period fabric prints, and furniture styles all allude to the belle Époque (without succumbing to chintz), but modern amenities and spacious-ness abound, thanks to the inn's true age (it was built in 1989). Put this within just min-utes' walk of all downtown, a beach, and four summer ferries, and its high-season rates (mid-June–August) compare favorably to all the equally expensive places purporting to swaddle their guests in luxuries. Come in the shoulder months, when rates drop $50 across the board, and you'll receive an even better bargain. Pets are welcomed in several of the rooms, too.

The strikingly beautiful **(Iroquois Cottage** (Samoset Ave., 508/693-3627 or 888/693-3627, www.narragansetthouse.com, May–Oct., $200–275 d), the sister property to the neighboring Narragansett House, was built as a Victorian guest house in the 1870s. Completely gut-renovated in the late 1990s, its six spacious, elegant guest rooms are a far cry from the 19th century's cramped and spartan lodgings. Now you'll enjoy luxury linens, ori-ental carpets, antiques, stained glass transoms, rich woodwork, fully modern baths, and pri-vate porches—plus the soundproofing afforded by modern construction. Rates, which are at their peak from Memorial Day through Labor Day, include a continental breakfast.

If want resort activities—tennis courts, swimming pool, proximity to golf and beaches—without paying a premium for 24-hour staff and room service, consider the **Island Inn** (Island Inn Ln. off Beach Rd.,

508/693-2002 or 800/462-0269, www.island inn.com, late Mar.–Oct., $210–245 d, dis-counts for stays of four days or more), about a mile and a half from downtown. The decor is comparable to modern motel rooms found along every interstate in the country, with com-fortable furnishings and forgettable framed art. However, there are also kitchenettes or full kitchens in every room. Families will ap-preciate the spacious two-bedroom suites and two-story townhouses ($285–375). Prices are at their peak only from late June–August, so even better deals may be had in the early or late days of summer. If you like traveling with your pet, note that outside of high season the inn also accepts canine companions, one of the few properties on the Vineyard to do so.

$250 and Up

At the quiet end of downtown, **The Oak Bluffs Inn** (Circuit Ave. and Pequot, 508/693-7171 or 800/955-6235, www.oakbluffsinn.com, May–Oct., $215–300 d) honors the town's decorative pedigree downstairs, but upstairs a soothing lack of Victoriana reigns, making the comfortable, high-ceilinged rooms seem even more spacious. A four-story tower with a rooftop cupola gives late-August guests a sky-box seat for the town's end-of-season fireworks display (and simply a great view at any time). The rates, which peak mid-June–Labor Day, do not include an 11 percent tax and "gratu-ity" surcharge.

(The Oak House (79 Seaview Ave., 508/693-4187 or 866/693-5805, www.vine yardinns.com, mid-May–Oct., $240–330 d) between Narragansett and Pequot is a former summer home of the state's fourth Republican governor. It's been turned into the quintessential B&B—a seaside Victorian with a picket fence and peaked roof, rocker-filled porches for after-noon tea and lemonade, and sunny balconies overlooking the beach across the street. Whether clad in solid oak paneling or coordinated around more feminine yellows and pinks, the 10 rooms and suites are almost exactly as you'd imagine a B&B should look, from antiques and gauzy curtains to the occasional painted brass bed or

Oriental rug. (They also come with TVs and telephones.) Two-room suites run $360–370 for up to four people in high season.

FOOD

When dyed-in-the-wool Nantucketers threaten their offspring with visions of the bogeyman, chowing down on pub grub on Oak Bluffs' Circuit Avenue is what they have in mind. But bars don't have a monopoly on this island's cheap eats. Instead, make your way to **Linda Jean's** (25 Circuit Ave., 508/693-4093, 6 A.M.–8 P.M. daily, $6.95–14.95), where sturdy breakfasts, lunches, and early dinners transport patrons back to simpler days and square meals, when coffee came only as decaf or regular and Cool Whip had cachet.

Hearty, thick-crusted pizza is available at **Giordano's Restaurant, Clam Bar & Pizza** (Circuit Ave., 508/693-0184, www.giosmv.com, 11:30 A.M.–10:30 P.M. daily late May–early Sept., $9.95–21.95, cash only) filling the entire block opposite the Flying Horses Carousel. But the real reason to come here is the robust and inexpensive red-sauce Italian meals. Another enjoyable, affordable Italian option—and the only one for off-season visitors—is **Pomodoro** (53 Circuit Ave., 508/696-3002, 11:30 A.M.–9:30 P.M. daily, $8.95–15.75), also serving up inexpensive pastas and pizzas in a high-ceilinged, contemporary space with a casual, family-friendly atmosphere.

Across the street is the ever-popular **◖ Slice of Life** (50 Circuit Ave., 508/693-3838, www.sliceoflifemv.com, 8 A.M.–9 P.M. daily, till 10 P.M. in summer, $7.50–22), a cozy little cafe and bakery featuring simple fare made from scratch with the best ingredients available. That means breakfast dishes with quality meats and cheeses (no bright orange American cheese slices here), buttermilk pancakes with real maple syrup, a flavorful lunch assortment of grilled panini, pizza, and salads, and dinner staples of roasted organic chicken, local fish, grilled or barbecued meats, and their lean half-pound burger on a rustic roll. Leave room for the scrumptious desserts.

OB is home to the island's sole brewpub,

the **Offshore Ale Company** (30 Kennebec Ave., 508/693-2626, www.offshoreale.com, 11:30 A.M.–close daily, $10.95–25.95), where a half-dozen housemade beers are always on tap. While the rustic building and peanut shells strewn on the plank flooring set the tone, the food is above average: generous salads, wood-fired brick-oven pizzas, hearty burgers cooked to order, fresh local oysters, beer-battered fish and chips, even a kid's menu. Come summer the Offshore also features live music four times a week, including a weekly Irish sessiun on Wednesday evening.

While there's no shortage of other taverns in town where you can slake your thirst for brews and burgers while ESPN plays on the TV over the bar, a special nod is due to **Seasons Eatery & Pub** (19 Circuit Ave., 508/693-7129, www.seasonspub.com, 11 A.M.–11 P.M. daily, $8.95–23.95). Beside the standard menu of burgers, sandwiches, chicken wings, salads, pasta, steak, and seafood, there's a full sushi bar incongruously adjacent to the main dining area. The extensive menu of maki rolls and nigiri pieces can be accompanied by cold sake, or just one of the nearly two dozen beers on tap at the regular bar. If there's a pro sport that you want watch while dining, this is a good place to come, as there are TVs just about everywhere you look. Kids get free tokens for the next-door game room with their meals, and if you couldn't leave your laptop at home, the place is a WiFi hotspot, too. Good thing there's so much else to do on the island or there might not be any reason to leave the premises.

The man behind the Seasons sushi concession has his own little restaurant nearby: **O-Sun Asian Kitchen** (5 Oak Bluffs Ave., 508/696-0220, 11 A.M.–9:30 P.M. daily, $11–28) mixes tasty Japanese noodle, rice, and tempura dishes with a modest menu of Chinese items, all at low prices not often seen on the Vineyard. The view from seats facing the windows takes in the nearby Steamship Authority pier, the long arm of Chappaquiddick on the horizon, and usually a handful of sailboats scudding across the bay in between.

OB has its high-end eateries, too. One of the

best is 🄲 **Park Corner Bistro** (20H Kennebec Ave., 508/696-9922, 5–10 P.M. daily June–Sept., hours vary Oct.–May, $15–28), fronting the small downtown Post Office plaza. "Bistro" here draws more inspiration from TriBeCa than Paris—behind the mullioned windows are a small dining room and even smaller bar, stylishly decorated with dark wood, white linens, black trim, and lithesome waitstaff. The casual air is all Vineyard, though, and the food is simply excellent: assertive flavors, novel touches (a lashing of bourbon in the pan of the pork tenderloin, a splash of citrus in the garlicky steamed mussel broth), homemade pastas, ample portions, and no skimping on the wine servings if you order by the glass. In summer, breakfast and a Latino-flavored lunch are served, too.

For a real splurge, try **The Sweet Life Café** (63 Circuit Ave., 508/696-0200, www.sweetlifemv.com, 5:30 P.M.–close Thurs.–Mon. May–mid-Oct. and 5:30 P.M.–close daily mid-June–early Sept., $32–44) opposite the Oak Bluffs Inn. The elegance and intimacy of the residential interior and back garden provide the perfect backdrop for the kitchen's contemporary approach to classic continental cuisine, pairing fine meats, fresh fish, and pick-of-the-crop vegetables with flavorful herbed broths, glazes, and wine reductions. Steak frites, braised monkfish with linguini and clams, an autumnal rack of pork in port wine sauce with pumpkin risotto, or wild mushroom strudel with polenta are just a few examples—each plate arranged with an painterly flourish. The expertise also extends to the desserts—life doesn't get any sweeter than this.

In a class by itself is **Lola's Southern Seafood** (15 Island Inn Rd., 508/693-5007, www.lolassouthernseafood.com, 5 P.M.–close Thurs.–Sat. and 10 A.M.–2 P.M. Sun. starting Easter weekend and ending late Oct., varied additional days in May and Sept., daily late May–early Sept., till 11 P.M. late June–Aug., lunch noon–3 P.M. Mon.–Sat. late June–early Sept., $19.95–39.95) at the Island Inn off Beach Road. Although it's a trek from downtown OB if you're on foot (it's easier to just hop the VTA bus 13 to Edgartown), Lola's gives you more than enough reason to need that 1.3-mile walk back to Ocean Park and the Steamship dock. Lola, who is from Louisiana, has abandoned the idea of portion control. Forget ordering a full entrée for every adult—each platter comes with enough side dishes (starches and greens) to choke a horse. Pony up the fee for splitting a plate (or stick to the appetizers), and you'll still pay less and eat more than in almost any other island restaurant. Anyone lacking a teamster's appetite may want to stick to the pub, where a saner sense of proportion prevails (think 7 rather than 16 ounces of steak, for instance, or a plate rather than a platter of jambalaya) with commensurately lower prices.

Edgartown

With more than 350 years of history, staid old Edgartown is the antipode of youthfully energetic adjacent Oak Bluffs, which is why skateboarders and in-line skaters should be aware of the $20 fine for venturing downtown on wheels. Yachting is the only true sport here, and if you can't afford to maintain a boat for the season, you can still adopt the local dress code of ruddy pink pants and brass-buttoned blue blazer—or a full outfit of tennis whites prior to cocktail hour—and pretend one of those sleek-hulled vessels swinging out there on its mooring is yours.

Called Great Harbor by the English (who made it their first island settlement) and then Old Town, after a second community was carved out of Indian lands to the west, Edgartown was renamed in tribute to the young son of the Duke of York and was finally incorporated in 1671, the same year the Duke gave his approval to Thomas Mayhew, Sr.'s private Manor of Tisbury. (Getting the ducal wink and nod was crucial—just a few years earlier, the restored Merry Monarch, King Charles II, had sown great confusion by giving the Duke's Manhattan-based colony nominal control over all the dry land off the southern New England coast, from Long Island to Nantucket.) The most enduring legacy of old Mayhew's rule is Edgartown's continuing role as the seat of regional government—named with anachronistic English pomp the "County of Dukes County" and comprising both Martha's Vineyard and the Elizabeth Islands. But the Lord of Tisbury might take a pacesetter's pride in the town's per-capita income (highest in the region) and feel a kinship with the town's many registered Republicans (the largest percentage on the island). For the visitor, however, probably more interesting than the modern abundance of country squires is the town's abundant neoclassical architecture—testament to the wealth accumulated by captains and ship owners in the heyday of whaling.

SIGHTS
Landmark Buildings
Three of the town's architectural treasures are owned by the Martha's Vineyard Preservation Trust, which maintains one as a museum and keeps all three open for scheduled seasonal tours. The Trust's headquarters occupy the **Daniel Fisher House** (99 Main St., 508/627-4440, www.mvpreservation.org), an elegant Federal-style mansion built in 1840 by one of the island's most successful whale-oil tycoons. Superb though its symmetry may be, the good Dr. Fisher's home was upstaged nine years later by his next-door neighbor, the **Old Whaling Church,** a Greek Revival eminence whose giant columns and broad pediment evoke the Parthenon's temple front. The Trust-owned building now does double duty as the Edgartown Performing Arts Center, with a broad variety of secular events complementing the Methodist services still conducted each Sunday beneath the graceful chandeliers. Befitting such a true community center, its 92-

foot clock tower is also a landmark for boaters out in Nantucket Sound.

In utilitarian contrast to this pair's grandeur is the **Vincent House** (11 A.M.–3 P.M. Mon.–Fri., May–Columbus Day, $4), a simple, south-facing example of early New England's homegrown "full Cape" style—i.e., a steep-roofed, story-and-a-half box with pairs of windows flanking a central door. Built in 1672, it's the island's oldest surviving residence and retains its original masonry, nails, hinges, handles, and woodwork. It's also the Preservation Trust's museum of island life. During the same season, guided tours of all three Trust properties are available daily on the hour at 11 A.M., noon, 1 P.M., and 2 P.M. for $10, starting from (and including admission to) the Vincent House. If you intend to also visit the Martha's Vineyard Museum, you can purchase a joint ticket ($15) valid for as many days as it takes for you to visit each property.

◖ Historic Downtown Edgartown
Streets intersecting Main near the center of town—School, Summer, Winter—are all worth roaming for a good look at the full range of island architectural styles, from old saltboxes and half-Capes to spare Congregational meetinghouses and Tiffany-windowed Catholic churches. But Water Street is the island's premiere showcase of Federal and Greek Revival styles. Wander in either direction, north or south, past the shops and the verandas of downtown inns and you'll quickly come to numerous 19th-century captains' and merchants' houses lined up along the harbor and looking, with their black shutters and white siding, like so many piano keys.

In this street-sized textbook of neoclassical architecture, you should have no trouble spotting either the restrained Federal style of the early 1800s (pilasters framing nearly square facades; columned porticos, fanlight windows and sometimes even sidelights framing the front doors; smaller third-story windows; and fancy, turned balustrades crowning flat roof lines) or the bold Greek columns of the successive style, which came into vogue following the widely reported expeditions of British Lord Elgin to Athens's Acropolis.

⟨ Edgartown Lighthouse

If downtown's concrete expressions of the 19th century's love of Greek and Roman civilization don't inspire noble resolutions to read your Ovid or Aeschylus, perhaps you'd prefer to sit at the base of the 20th-century Edgartown Lighthouse at the end of North Water Street and entertain more modern sentiments about the inconstancy of sun and tide. By the time the cast-iron present tower was brought, early in World War II, to replace its 111-year-old predecessor, shifting sand had filled in around what originally was a stone pier set a short way from shore; where once the lighthouse keeper had to row to his post, now you may simply stroll through salt-spray roses.

Still an aid to navigation owned by the U.S. Coast Guard, the lighthouse is maintained by the Martha's Vineyard Museum. Renovated in 2007 to finally outfit the interior with stairs (previously, access to the top was only by ladder), the top of the light is open to the public 11 A.M.–5 P.M. Thursday–Monday ($5), with hours extended on Thursday to 30 minutes after sunset.

Martha's Vineyard Museum

Comprising a collection of buildings a couple blocks from downtown's commercial bustle, the Martha's Vineyard Museum (508/627-4441, www.mvmuseum.org, 10 a.m.–5 p.m. Mon.–Sat. mid-June–Columbus Day, 10 a.m.–4 p.m. the rest of the year, $7 in season and $6 off season) is fortunate to possess a better-than-average potpourri of historical relics—over 30,000 in all, from scrimshaw and whaling try-pots to costumes, domestic furnishings, and old farm implements. The Martha's Vineyard Historical Society curates the museum, mining this repository of artifacts for its changing exhibits, and also drawing upon the society's vast collection of historical photos, vintage postcards, and ephemera. Genealogists who fancy some connection to past islanders should visit the

Edgartown Lighthouse is a popular spot for weddings and parties.

society's library to research the family tree. The library also sells copies of the Dukes County Intelligencer, the society's quarterly assemblage of articles on island history and lore.

The museum's most prominent exhibit is visible even before entering through the corner gatehouse—sitting in the yard is a large piece of lighthouse technology over 140 years old, an example of the huge Fresnel lens, whose invention revolutionized coastal navigation. The ground-level view from inside the lens may seem disorienting, but these concentric prisms totally reversed the illuminating efficiency of 19th-century lamps; whereas before, only one-sixth of a parabolic reflector's light could be seen by mariners, Augustin Fresnel's "dioptric apparatus" concentrated as much light in its high-powered beam as had previously been lost. In a reminder that red-tape bureaucracy is hardly a modern affliction, the U.S. government dithered for 30 years, despite the proven efficiency, making scientific studies and committee reports before finally adopting the French-made lens. One of the earliest Fresnels

ODE TO A VINEYARD CHICKEN

If you visit the Vineyard Museum in Edgartown, be sure to pause a moment and pay your respects at the two verse-covered headstones in the Carriage House. Nancy Luce, the West Tisbury woman who had these memorials erected before she died in 1890, would surely appreciate the visit. And so, no doubt, would the bantam hens honored by the tablets: Ada Queetie, Beauty Linna, and Poor Tweedle Dedel Bebbee Pinky.

Poor little Ada Queetie,
She always used to want to get in my lap
And squeeze me close up, and talk
pretty talk to me.
She always used to want I should hug
her up close to my face,
And keep still there she loved me so well.
When she used to be in her little box to
lay pretty egg,
She would peak up from under the chair,
To see her friendy's face.

Poor little Ada Queetie has departed
this life,
Never to be here no more,
No more to love, no more to speak,
No more to be my friend,
O how I long to see her with me, live
and well,
Her heart and mine united,
Love and feelings deeply rooted for
each other,
She and I could never part,
I am left broken hearted.

Luce was one of the island's best-known "characters," an eccentric who wrote a volume of poetry, *Poor Little Hearts,* for her beloved chickens. She sold copies of the book – and postcards of her brood – to 19th-century tourists who passed her farm (she also happily gave recitals for a small tip). Her own grave, toward the rear of the West Tisbury burying ground, off State Road, bears a simple marker without any epitaph.

installed by the U.S. Lighthouse Service, this particular lens faithfully flashed its light over Aquinnah for nearly a century before it was replaced by an electric lamp.

During the off-season, one of the major display areas—the Thomas Cooke House, that tidy 18th-century Colonial—is closed for lack of heating.

Chappaquiddick

The Wampanoags' descriptive name for Edgartown's sibling chunk of tree-covered sand means "separated island," but modern inhabitants have no time for all those syllables; it's "Chappy" now, to one and all. But the full name endures in infamy after what happened in 1969, when a car accident proved fatal to a young woman and nearly so to the career of the state's then-junior senator, who was behind the wheel. Kennedy-bashing may be a popular recreation back where you come from, but not here; nothing brands a visitor as an off-island

yahoo more quickly than chasing after vicious gossip about the nation's foremost political dynasty. Of course, plenty of Islanders privately suspect that tourists are all yahoos anyway, so questions about what happened that night in '69 are grudgingly anticipated.

Sparsely inhabited and infused with rural end-of-the-road isolation, Chappy feels far off the map even when the waiting line at the ferry clearly proves the opposite. Visitors are lured by the superb beaches at Wasque and Cape Poge, but canoeing, bird-watching, bodysurfing, surf-casting, hiking, and walking are equally good reasons to join that ferry line.

Means of access to the island (which isn't quite separated anymore) are limited to the **Chappy Ferry,** a.k.a. the *"On Time"* (508/627-9427, $12 for cars and drivers, $6 for bikes and riders, $4 pedestrians), or a good swim across the narrow entrance to Edgartown's inner harbor. The ferry runs every day of the year from the waterfront downtown, beginning at 6:45 A.M. Rates and schedule are posted at the landings, but in brief, you can count on continuous service until midnight in season (May 15–Oct. 15), and until 7 P.M. otherwise; after 7:30 P.M. off season, two periods of service are spread out over the evening with the final run leaving at 11:10 P.M. All fares are round-trip and are collected in full upon first crossing. Because of the maze of narrow one-way streets approaching the Edgartown waterfront, even bicyclists should follow the Chappy Ferry signs.

FARM Institute

The Vineyard is fortunate to have a number of dedicated individuals and organizations trying to raise awareness about the importance of preserving local farms. With homes being built at an annual rate of nearly five per week, there is unceasing pressure to turn the island's remaining agricultural land into house lots. With an eye on changing the perception of agricultural land and labor through education, the FARM Institute (Aero Ave., 508/627-7007, www.farminstitute.org) uses hands-on activities to teach kids the value of sustainable food production, responsibility for caring for and raising farm animals, and stewardship of land for the benefit of the community. Pretty radical stuff for 21st-century kids raised on Wii and fast food. Judging by the endless smiles on the faces of the young farmer-campers who lend a hand to help run the place, this 160-acre working farm is nurturing a bumper crop of educated consumers and policy-makers for the future, along with chemical-free meat and produce for local restaurants and markets.

If you are staying on the island for at least a week between June and August with a child between the ages of 5 and 14, visit the institute's website to download a program brochure describing the farm's rolling series of Monday–Friday half- and full-day summer camps and teen apprentice programs ($300–410, with discounts for early registration). There are also two-day, 90-minute programs for two- to four-year-olds ($60). On the second and fourth Saturdays of July and August the farm welcomes volunteers of all ages to help feed animals, col-

kids feeding the free-range chickens at the FARM Institute

lect eggs, work in the barn and garden, and perform other necessary farm chores.

You came to the island to play, not pick vegetables or care for piglets? No problem, the Institute has that covered, too, with its five-acre corn maze (dawn–dusk daily mid-July–Sept., $10 ages 14 and up, $5 otherwise). The farm's master maze designer is a wizard at crafting a challenging course, which each year is divided into two routes. One, aimed at beginners, is estimated to take under 30 minutes to complete, while the second, more advanced route is intended to keep you busy for over an hour.

The FARM Institute is located on the right side of Katama Road on the way to Edgartown's South Beach, about 1.6 miles from the fork with Herring Creek Road.

ENTERTAINMENT

Diverse is the adjective for Edgartown's **Performing Arts Center** (89 Main St., 508/627-4442), in the Old Whaling Church, whose calendar typically ranges from big names in acoustic and spoken performance to antiques auctions and assorted other community events. One regular on the church schedule is the **Martha's Vineyard Chamber Music Society** (508/696-8055), whose series of weekly concerts in July and August are performed on Monday nights in Edgartown, and then on Tuesday at the **Chilmark Community Center** (520 South Rd. in Chilmark, 508/645-9484, www.chilmarkcommunitycenter.org).

Nightlife

The Vineyard's biggest club and the only one that attracts national touring rock, reggae, funk, jazz, fusion, and folk acts sits out on the airport entrance road: **Outerland** (17 Airport Rd., 508/693-1137, www.outerlandmv.com, schedule varies late May–Sept.). The former hangar was made famous in the '80s as a low-rent tin-roofed dive featuring intimate performances by friends and contemporaries of then–co-owner Carly Simon.

After passing through other hands and eventually into bankruptcy, the club was resurrected by local luminaries whose collective influence ensures that big-name performers continue to make use of the state-of-the-art stage and sound system behind the deliberately nondescript metal exterior and wall-sized evocation of Thomas Hart Benton's Vineyard paintings. An outpost of Oak Bluffs' Smoke 'n' Bones Bar-B-Q dishes up finger-licking southern-style ribs, brisket, catfish, and other omnivorous treats 6–9:30 P.M. whenever there's a show (the music typically starts at 10 P.M.). Handicap-accessible and smoke-free, the place also offers memberships if you want to avoid being excluded by the guardians of the gate.

SHOPPING

Despite Edgartown's high-end demographics and an affected gentility unsullied by crass neon and billboards, each new season seems to find another of the city's expensive boutiques turning into another T-shirt shop indistinguishable from those found in every tourist town the world over. Holdouts against this trend include one of the island's most prominent galleries, plus a few purveyors of eye-catching, offbeat, or just plain unique gifts and indulgences.

While you'll find the most interesting gift and souvenir shopping around the harbor, long-term visitors on errands in cars prefer the commercial plazas on Upper Main Street between the Stop & Shop and The Triangle (the local name for the split between Main and the roads to Vineyard Haven and Oak Bluffs). The narrow, one-way downtown streets are great for pedestrians, but summer drivers should take an extra dose of hypertension medication before trying to do the same.

Foremost among the harborfront art venues is the **Old Sculpin Gallery** (58 Dock St., 508/627-4881, www.oldsculpingallery.org, 9 A.M.–9 P.M. Mon.–Sat., noon–8 P.M. Sun. late May–mid-Oct.) opposite the ramp for the Chappy Ferry. Housed in a former boatbuilders' workshop, this is the Vineyard's oldest operating gallery, run by the nonprofit Martha's Vineyard Art Association. The MVAA also operates their Studio School in the building, offering art classes and workshops for kids, teens, and adults throughout the summer; email mvaa@verizon.net for registration details. Drop by for a snack and a sip with the artists at the customary new show openings, every Sunday evening from 6 P.M. till closing.

A block up from the harbor is the **Christina Gallery** (32 N. Water St., 508/627-8794 or 800/648-1815, www.christina.com, 10 A.M.–5 P.M. daily Apr.–Dec., hours vary Jan.–March). The two floors of paintings and photographs are often quite predictable, but venture upstairs past all the sun-drenched beach, cottage, and sailing scenes and you'll find a trove of antique charts and maps.

Don't miss **Once in a Blue Moon** (12 N. Summer St., www.bluemoonmv.com, 508/627-9177, 10 A.M.–5:30 P.M. daily late May–Sept., hours vary off season, closed Jan.–Apr.), for its stunning yet affordable jewelry, much of it handcrafted contemporary work from predominantly European artists. The unique designs are complemented by other selected works of fine art, as well as one-of-a-kind women's clothing and fashion accessories.

© KATHRYN OSGOOD

Tom Demont, owner and artist of Edgartown Scrimshaw Gallery, working on a custom engraving

Next door is **The Golden Door** (18 N. Summer St., www.thegoldendoormv.com, 508/627-7740, 9 A.M.–5 P.M. daily May–Oct., hours vary in the off-season), specializing in art from the Far East. It isn't nearly as incongruous as you might think—carved pachyderms, shining Buddhas, and mandala-like print fabrics were just the sort of worldly souvenirs whaling captains brought home a century and a half ago.

Crew members on those 19th-century whalers usually couldn't afford fancy trinkets for the loved ones *they* left behind. To keep from returning empty-handed, they used slack time over the course of their three- or four-year voyages to produce handmade gifts of scrimshaw, or carved whale ivory. The **Edgartown Scrimshaw Gallery** (43 Main St., 508/627-9439, 10:30 A.M.–5 P.M. Mon.–Sat. and 10:30 A.M.–4:30 P.M. Sun. June–Oct., 10:30 A.M.–5 P.M. Tues.–Sat. Nov.–Christmas and Apr.–May, and 11 A.M.–4 P.M. Sat. Jan.–Mar.) offers both antique and modern examples of the scrimshander's art (practiced these days mostly on the fossilized tusks of Siberian wooly mammoths, American mastodons, and walruses). Nantucket lightship baskets, lightship basket jewelry, wooden whales, and nautical art also fill the walls and cases of this shop, and friendly commentary is freely dispensed to the curious.

Whaling tales of a different sort—plus sailing stories and all manner of island-related reading matter—are found across the street in **Edgartown Books** (44 Main St., 508/627-8841, www.edgartownbooks.net, 9:30 A.M.–5:30 P.M. Mon.–Sat., 11 A.M.–4 P.M. Sun.), knowledgeable suppliers of good reading for beach chairs drawn into the shade or armchairs drawn up to the fire.

RECREATION
Beaches
When it comes to public beaches, Edgartown is arguably the most well endowed on the island, with surf of all sizes and miles of sand. Plenty of athletic-looking, bronze-bodied young surfers and swimmers make **South Beach** the Vineyard's answer to Southern California, although easy access from town ensures that

© KATHRYN OSGOOD

South Beach, also called Katama Beach, is three miles of barrier beach.

everybody can see and be seen on this lively three-mile strand. (By the way, the security guard at the far western end of the beach should convince anyone skeptical of the idea that some islanders enforce their waterfront property rights rather rigidly; he no longer packs a sidearm, but that's a small improvement.)

Swimmers who don't want to battle the undertow may prefer the warmer waters of Katama Bay, accessible from **Norton Point,** the narrow barrier that divides bay from ocean at the eastern end of the beach, or **Katama Point Preserve,** a small, sandy chunk of Land Bank property adjacent to the town landing on Edgartown Bay Road. County-owned Norton Point, by the way, is the only part of the Vineyard outside of Chappaquiddick that allows driving on the beach. Required oversand vehicle permits ($30/day or $100 for Apr. 1–Mar. 31, discounts for county residents) are available from the Treasurer's Office (9 Airport Rd., 508/696-3845), or in summer at South Beach at the Norton Point gatehouse.

Facing Nantucket Sound on the combined outer shores of Chappy's Cape Poge Wildlife Refuge and Wasque Reservation, **East Beach** and **Chappaquiddick State Beach**—still known to many locals as Leland Beach—constitute Edgartown's other breathtaking waterfront. Over four miles of austere, unspoiled barrier beach backed by fragile grass-covered dunes, salt marsh, and salt ponds await swimmers and beach walkers. Swimmers should stay far from the Point itself due to the dangerous riptides.

Expect to pay admission in season ($3 adults, free for ages 15 and under, May 30–Oct. 15), and expect to find some bird-nesting areas roped off in summer. Each end of the shore has its own access point: the northern end via Dike Road, and the southern end at Wasque Point. Oversand vehicle permits are a flat $180, valid for a year (Apr. 1–Mar. 31), and may be purchased 9 A.M.–5 P.M. daily May 30–October 15 from the Wasque Reservation gatehouse (508/627-3255), the Dike Bridge gatehouse (508/627-3599), or from a patrolling ranger. Out of season the permits are available from the Trustees of Reservations office in Vineyard Haven (860 State Rd., 508/693-7662), or from Coop's Bait & Tackle in Edgartown (147 West Tisbury Rd., 508/627-3909, about a mile from Main Street).

Anyone seeking an escape to the water within easy walking distance of downtown should consider **Chappy Point Beach,** a narrow outer harbor strip of sand on Chappaquiddick, within a short stroll of the *"On Time"* ferry. Flanking the squat tower of Edgartown Light on Starbuck Neck are two more beaches—**Lighthouse** and **Fuller Street**—half a mile of mostly sand, weather depending, as suited to views of the historic Edgartown Inn or close-up portraits of the lighthouse as to sunbathing or swimming.

Private property ownership prevents anyone on South Beach from venturing farther west, but there is in fact a short amount of public beach on the barrier dunes between the ocean and Edgartown Great Pond. Owned by the Land Bank and named, appropriately enough, **Edgartown Great Pond Beach,** the property is only accessible by boat, which can only be put in at the Turkeyland Cove town landing on the Great Pond (all ponds of sufficient size are public waterways). This landing is at the end of an unsignposted dirt turnoff from Meetinghouse Road just opposite the white fence marked 145. From the West Tisbury–Edgartown Road, it's 1.3 miles south on Meetinghouse to the turnoff (the only one with a Y on the right side of the road), and another 0.8 miles to the actual landing; if coming from Road to the Plains, it's 0.2 miles north on Meetinghouse to the turnoff. After you've set out by boat, aim for the left side of the barrier beach and watch for the Land Bank's boundary-marking signs.

Water Sports

Sengekontacket Pond, shared between Oak Bluffs and Edgartown, is an excellent spot for windsurfers, kayakers, and canoers. Although Sengekontacket can get too shallow at really low tides, it typically has steady winds and is free of motorized craft. Access is from the boat ramps off of Beach Road. Strong currents and prevailing offshore winds make Cow Bay (in front of State Beach) and enclosed Katama Bay (accessible from the town boat ramp on Katama Bay Road in Edgartown) the province of more experienced windsurfers and paddlers.

Whether you bring your own boat or the means to transport a rental, you'll find several fine saltwater and freshwater ponds worth exploring, including Poucha Pond, at Wasque Reservation, and Edgartown Great Pond, via the Turkeyland Cove town landing off Meetinghouse Road.

Guided canoe outings (including canoe) are scheduled in summer by the **Massachusetts Audubon Society** (508/627-4850, www .massaudubon.org), and the **Trustees of Reservations** (508/627-3599, www.thetrust ees.org), at Felix Neck and Cape Poge Wildlife Sanctuaries, respectively.

◖ Sailing Katama Bay

In 2007 a storm cut through the barrier beach at the southern end of Katama Bay, roiling Edgartown's formerly mild-mannered Katama Bay with steady, occasionally swift currents previously quite alien to the well-protected inner harbor. Despite the new challenges to slipping in and out of docks—which could last for decades before the breach is naturally sealed, as hydrographers predict—Edgartown remains one of southern New England's most popular sailing spots. You, too, can experience the beautiful bay and adjacent outer harbor waters off Cape Poge with one of the sailing vessels that call this town home.

For scheduled outings, contact **Mad Max Sailing Adventures** (25 Dock St., 508/627-7500, www.madmaxmarina.com, 2 and 6 P.M. daily late May–early Sept., call for schedule through Oct. 1, $55), which offers daily two-hour cruises, rain or shine, aboard its sleek 60-foot catamaran. Or consider the *Magic Carpet* (Memorial Wharf, 508/645-2889 or 627-2889, www.sailmagiccarpet.com, daily June–early Oct., $65), a beautiful all-wood teak and mahogany European-built 56-foot Bermudan yawl designed by Sparkman and Stephens, naval architects renowned for their racing yachts. Join this pedigreed former New York Yacht Club flagship for two-hour public sails four times a day from morning till sunset. Calling on short notice—even the same day—is perfectly acceptable, given that you may change your mind about sailing in uncertain weather, although reservations are preferred. Both accept bookings for private sails, too. Bring your own snacks and beverages, alcoholic or otherwise.

Felix Neck Wildlife Sanctuary

This Massachusetts Audubon Society property (Felix Neck Dr., 508/627-4850, www.mass audubon.org, trails daily dawn to dusk, $4) lies on a neck of land jutting out into Sengekontacket Pond, a large windsurfer and waterfowl habitat whose saltwater ebbs and flows with the tides in adjacent Cow Bay. A good cross section of the Vineyard's landscape is found here, from open meadows to woodlands. There's a small freshwater pond attractive to black ducks and mallards, and a bird blind to make their nesting and feeding easier to watch. Similarly, patient observers can spy on the spring nesting of fast-diving ospreys—also known as buzzards—atop poles strategically placed in the open margin of the peninsula's pine groves.

Throughout summer and fall, there are various scheduled walks with naturalists to introduce you to the sanctuary's wildflowers, birds, turtles, and marine life. Other program highlights include canoe trips, stargazing, snorkeling in Sengekontacket Pond, and even cruises to the Elizabeth Islands. Ask at the nature center (8:30 A.M.–4:30 P.M. Mon.–Fri., 9:30 A.M.–4:30 P.M. Sat., and 10 A.M.–3 P.M. Sun. June–Aug.; 9 A.M.–4 P.M. Mon.–Fri., 10 A.M.–3 P.M. Sat., and 12:30–3 P.M. Sun. Sept.–May) about these and other current activities.

The entrance is a sandy lane signposted on the Edgartown–Vineyard Haven Road.

North Neck Highlands Preserve

One of the least strenuous, yet most rewarding hikes is found at this diminutive Land Bank parcel, where one side of Chappy narrows to the point of being just some hundreds of yards in width. From the first parking lot, a short trail west leads to a sharp bluff with panoramic views over Edgartown Harbor, the lighthouse, State Beach, Oak Bluffs, and the long thin arc of Cape Poge Elbow. Wooden stairs descend to the narrow beach below, with benches helpfully placed on the way down. When the beach is in the lee of the prevailing breeze, a remarkable stillness may be found here—and since swimming is not allowed, the quiet is usually only shared with folks casting lines into the narrow gut through which Cape Poge Pond empties into the harbor. The eastern side of the preserve lies along the much rougher, rockier pond shore. Both sides afford fine bird-watching, as migrating species take a rest in the preserve's low, scrubby trees after crossing Vineyard Sound. Access to the property is along a very bumpy sand road—North Neck Road—a little over a mile from Chappaquiddick Road, and a total of about 2.5 miles from the Chappy Ferry.

◖ Mytoi

Midway along Chappaquiddick's sandy Dike Road, the scaly trunks and tangled branches of pitch pine suddenly give way to the improbable sight of a little Japanese-style garden. The creation of Mary Wakeman, a well-known local conservationist, Mytoi is now one of the small gems in the crown of the Trustees of Reservations (www.thetrustees.org). The garden exudes tranquility. Even at the zenith of summer, the pond inspires philosophical thoughts; cross the arched bridge to the islet at its center and feel them rise up like morning light. In spring—when the slopes are blanketed with bold daffodils, rhododendrons, dogwood, azaleas, and roses—the windswept, beach-grass-covered dunes at the end of the road might as well be halfway around the world. Though entry is free, contributions toward the site's upkeep are encouraged (note the metal dropbox before you get to the pond). A water fountain and restroom provide amenities rarely found on such rural properties; also, take advantage of the recycling bins for disposing of those empty cans and bottles rolling around your backpack or back seat.

◖ Wasque Point and Cape Poge

The Trustees of Reservations also own nearly the entire east shore of Chappaquiddick, from the southern end of Katama Bay to Cape Poge Bay, from whose waters are taken some 50 percent of the state's annual bay scallop harvest. **Cape Poge Wildlife Refuge** encompasses over four miles of this barrier beach, accessible via Dike Bridge at the end of Dike Road, while **Wasque Reservation** (WAY-skwee) protects a couple more miles of dunes and grassland around Wasque Point. Admission to either or both is $3 (free for ages 15 and under, $3 parking June–Sept., parking free the rest of the year). Restrooms, drinking water, and recycling bins for beverage containers are all found at Wasque; at Dike Bridge there is nothing but a pay phone beside the attendant's shack.

Oversand vehicle permits are necessary for driving beyond the Cape Poge parking area ($180, valid Apr. 1–Mar. 31). Purchase from gatehouse attendant 9 A.M.–5 P.M. daily May 30–Oct. 15, or from a patrolling ranger. Out of season the permits are available from the Trustees of Reservations office in Vineyard Haven (860 State Rd., 508/693-7662), or from Coop's Bait & Tackle in Edgartown (147 West Tisbury Rd., 508/627-3909, a little over a mile from Main Street). Air for reinflating tires is available year-round at Mytoi. Even with the requisite permit, be aware that access may be totally denied if the endangered piping plover and least tern are nesting on the beach. The dunes are quite fragile, anchored by those wisps of beachgrass; since destabilized dunes are more likely to wash or blow away—or choke up the salt marsh that helps support the rich shellfish beds—you'll notice many warnings posted to stay on existing Jeep tracks and boardwalks. If you hate having your freedom circumscribed by such silly-sounding restrictions, be warned that nature is the enforcer here as much as any ranger—the beachgrass is riddled with poison ivy.

The summer crowds come mostly for the swimming and surf fishing (beware of the undertow), but any time of year, this shore is unmatched for the simple pleasure of walking until there's nothing but breaking waves and scuttling little sanderlings to keep you company. Bird-watching has gained a steady following, too, with osprey nesting on the pole at the northern end of the refuge, great blue herons stalking crabs through the tidal pools behind the dunes, oystercatchers foraging with their flashy orange bills at the edge of the surf, and ragged formations of sea ducks skimming across the winter ocean. The cedar-covered portions of Cape Poge provide browse for deer and small mammals, most of whom remain out of sight but for the occasional footprint or scat pile; if you're lucky, you may catch a glimpse of one of the resident sea otters slipping into a pond on the way up to the 1893 **Cape Poge Light.**

Thanks to the unremitting erosion along Chappaquiddick's outer shore, this is the Vineyard's most transient lighthouse; the present wooden tower has already been moved three times in the last century, most recently in 1986. Before it was automated in World War II, this lonely post was one of the many spoils available to the political party controlling the White House; whenever the presidency changed hands, so, too, would the nation's lighthouses. (Cape Poge's first keeper was appointed by Thomas Jefferson.)

Ninety-minute **lighthouse tours** are offered between Memorial Day and Columbus Day (daily at 9 A.M., noon, and 2 P.M., $25 adults and $12 kids). The beacon is also included on 2.5-hour **Cape Poge natural history tours** (508/627-3599, 9 A.M. and 2 P.M. daily Memorial Day–Columbus Day, $40 adults and $18 kids). Trustee members receive discounts on both trips. Joining the Trustees also makes it possible to sign up for the members-only **fishing discovery tours** out to a selected stretch of either Cape Poge or Wasque, where a fishing guide will teach you to surf cast (8:30 A.M. and 1:30 P.M. daily Memorial Day–Columbus Day, $60 adults and $25 kids). Special half-priced membership is available on the spot for anyone not yet belonging to the Trustees. Preregistration is required for all of these—space is limited. All three tours use special "safari" vehicles that depart from the Mytoi parking area (free van shuttle from the Chappy side of the *"On Time"* ferry).

Naturalist-guided canoe trips around Cape Poge Bay or Poucha Pond (POACH-a) are another option, priced and scheduled exactly the same as the natural history tours. Members-only **canoe rentals** (9 A.M.–5 P.M. daily June–Sept., $25 per half day and $35 per full eight-hour day) are also available for the do-it-yourselfer at the Dike Bridge gatehouse for use in Poucha Pond. Here again, would-be renters can instantly obtain special half-price Trustees' memberships.

Flying

Katama Airfield, off Edgartown's Herring Creek Road, is the nation's largest all-grass airfield. Established in 1924, its three runways see quite a bit of use from small private planes. It's also where you'll find **Martha's Vineyard Glider Rides** (508/627-3833 or 800/762-7464, www.800soaring.com, Mon.–Fri. early July–early Sept., $65–140 depending on the length of the ride), the island affiliate of Soaring Adventures of America, a national outfit with 150 locations coast to coast. On clear days, your enthusiastic pilots, Rob Wilkinson and Bob Stone, will give you a gull's-eye view of the Vineyard from a self-propelled sailplane or motorglider.

More airborne thrills are available from **Biplane Rides by Classic Aviators Ltd.** (508/627-7677, www.biplanemv.com, $149–399 for two depending on length of ride), offering open-cockpit flights in a Waco-UPF-7 acrobatic biplane. Loops, dives, barrel rolls, and other aerobatic maneuvers can be included for an extra fee.

When you return to earth, stop in at **The Right Fork Diner,** the airfield's diner, for a burger and fries, a taste of the owner's sweet rolls—from her grandmother's recipe—or just some Ben & Jerry's ice cream.

ACCOMMODATIONS

When it comes to accommodations, Edgartown costs more than any of its neighbors—witness the $300 summer rates for standard doubles in the island's only chain hotel. As a result the only time you will find rooms in the $100–150 range (or lower) is November through April.

$150-250

Located at the quiet edge of downtown, the **Edgartown Commons** (Pease's Point Way, 508/627-4671 or 800/439-4671, www.edgartowncommons.com, May–mid-Oct., $195–235 d, two-bedroom units $290–315) targets families seeking affordable lodgings with its 35 guest rooms—ranging from studio units to one- and two-bedroom suites—all featuring fully equipped kitchen areas. There is an outdoor pool and playground on the premises. Note that there is no air conditioning in any of the units—fans are provided instead—and there is no maid service, either.

$250-350

Stately old Edgartown has a number of large, luxurious inns carved out of elegant 19th-century homes. For example, canopy beds abound at **The Victorian Inn** (24 S. Water St., 508/627-4784, www.thevic.com, $255–425 d), which captures the spirit of its namesake era in both decor and in the utter absence of any TVs or phones. (WiFi, however, is available.) Thoroughly contemporary, however, is the dedication of the hands-on owners and well-trained staff to your comfort and enjoyment of the island, from the complimentary cut-glass decanter of vintage sherry in your room to an ever-ready willingness to help make arrangements for whatever sport or diversion suits your fancy. As for the generous four-course gourmet breakfasts, they are topped only by the views from the third-floor private balconies overlooking the garden court and harbor beyond the timeshare resort across the street. Predictably, rates peak between Memorial Day and Columbus Day; for real bargains visit in winter.

More of a B&B-style warm welcome is featured opposite the Old Whaling Church at the **Jonathan Munroe House** (100 Main St., 508/627-5536 or 877/468-6763, www.jona thanmunroe.com, $200–285 d). Its handful of generously sized rooms (half with fireplaces and whirlpool tubs), ample full breakfasts (choose from four entrées), afternoon wine and cheese, and dedicated staff offer year-round comfort. Like nearly every comparable property around, Jonathan Munroe House has a two- or three-night minimum in season. A snug two-floor, one-bedroom cottage in the rear garden, with fireplace and whirlpool bath, is a relative bargain at $375 d in summer.

The **Ashley Inn** (129 Main St., 508/627-9655 or 800/477-9655, www.ashleyinn.net, $250–375 d) occupies a shipshape old captain's home opposite small Cannonball Park. Rooms in the main house are a comfortable size (no tripping over your traveling companion's belongings) with unpretentious, tasteful decor; wonderfully friendly innkeepers; TVs and telephones; and a huge yard that invites curling up in the hammock with summer reading, far from the madding crowd. Prices are of course lower before June and after Columbus Day, bottoming out at $125–195 January–April; the three-night minimum only applies to high-season weekends, too. One- and two-bedroom townhouse suites with whirlpool tubs are also available by the week for anyone wishing to lie in the lap of luxury.

Plenty of elbow room comes standard at ❰ **The Lightkeepers Inn** (25 Simpson's Ln., 508/627-4600 or 800/946-3400, www .thelightkeepersinn.com, $275–375), whose five suites and private cottage are all large enough to include a queen four-poster bed, double pull-out sofa, and kitchen or kitchenette with dining area. (Room #3, the smallest, has a single-burner electric range, microwave, and mini-fridge rather than a full-sized four-hob range oven and refrigerator.) A family of four will find this place to be one of the best deals going given how few accommodations on the island have rooms designed with more than just couples in mind. If you find yourself stuck indoors, the pleasant and comfortable furnishings include TV, DVD, CD-radio,

and WiFi, and one upstairs suite has a delightful umbrella-shaded deck with charcoal grill. The inn manages to feel sequestered from the town's summer bustle even though it is located steps from downtown's shops and restaurants, and just a block and half from the harbor.

Nineteenth-century antiques aren't out of place at **The Shiverick Inn** (5 Pease's Point Way, 508/627-3797 or 800/723-4292, www .shiverickinn.com, $270–375 d, suites up to $550), one of the state's relatively rare Second Empire mansions, although the mansard roof and cupola are actually additions to the original 1840 house. The grace and simple refinement of that earlier age are borne out in the high-ceilinged rooms, cozy library, and formal gardens—where one may take one's afternoon tea (or morning granola, toast, and fruit) when weather allows. The inn's many fireplaces make it a romantic winter retreat (Nov.–Apr. rates start at under $140 d); but even in summer, its modest size and the innkeeper's deft personal touch keep the high-season pandemonium at bay.

The only national chain represented on the Islands is the modern **Clarion Martha's Vineyard** (227 Upper Main St., 508/627-5161 or 800/922-3009, www.clarionmv.com, $279–379 d). The full-sized, two-bed, air-conditioned rooms are exactly what you'd find nationwide. The prices, however, are all Vineyard.

$350 and Up

An atmosphere of relaxed but graceful welcome infuses the parlor registration area of the ❰ **Hob Knob Inn** (128 Main St., 508/627-9510 or 800/696-2723, www.hobknob.com, $350–525 d, suite $600). Thanks in part to the country decor, there is neither starched nor flowery formality here. Instead, wicker chairs and rockers on the wraparound porch and comfy seating in the common rooms invite guests to socialize or simply hang out as if visiting the manorial seat of some posh but down-to-earth godparent. The staff are clearly pros—warmly courteous, efficient, and prepared at the drop of a pin to help make your stay positively memorable. The individually-decorated rooms are larger than average and equipped with air purifiers and white-noise generators in addition to such standard amenities as flat-panel TVs, WiFi, terrycloth robes, and high-end bath amenities. Generous made-to-order breakfasts are included, and there are sauna, fitness, and spa facilities on the premises. You can rent bicycles on site, too.

Providing the perfect backdrop to the beachfront view of the Edgartown Lighthouse, the **Harbor View Hotel & Resort** (131 N. Water St., 508/627-7000 or 800/225-6005, www.harbor-view.com, $375–700 d, suites $780–1,600) is the epitome of a classic Gilded Age seaside resort. Built in 1891, its Shingle-style sprawl of turrets, wood railings, gables, and wide verandas looks like something out of *The Great Gatsby*. After nearly $80 million in renovations, the grand dame is once again a trendsetter in the Vineyard hotel business. In addition to high-end bath products and furnishings in all of its rooms and suites, it earns its place at the summit of local luxury properties with an emphasis on concierge services and activities programs for everyone in the family. From breakfast in bed to champagne on ice upon arrival, and from pilates classes on the lawn to fishing charters aboard the hotel's own boat, the Harbor View can pamper like no other.

FOOD

It's an old bit of folk wisdom that when you come across a botanical hazard in nature, the antidote is always growing nearby. Lo and behold, the same principle applies to the cost of eating out on the Vineyard. The ◖ **Dock St. Coffee Shop** (2 Dock St., 508/627-5232, 7 A.M.–10 P.M. daily year-round), a.k.a. the Dock Street Diner, is the island's hole-in-the-wall antidote to wallet-emptying restaurant prices—right in the heart of Edgartown, no less, next to R. W. Cutler's Bike Rentals at the very foot of Main Street. Postcards from customers taped to the soda fountain machine, out-of-date calendars on the wall, newspapers lying around on the counter, tasty breakfasts

for two for $10 before tip, and even decent frappes—see, there is a God.

Good-quality takeout, sit-down lunches, baked treats, and liquid refreshments are best obtained from **Espresso Love** (17 Church St., 508/627-9211, 8 A.M.–9 P.M. daily year-round), behind the County Court House on Main Street. Vegetarians will find that the **Edgartown Deli** (52 Main St., 508/627-4789, 8 A.M.–9 P.M. daily May–Oct.) makes a fine garden burger, and subscribers to the banana ice cream diet won't want to miss adjacent **Vineyard Scoops.** Fried seafood fans, meanwhile, should step down to the takeout-only **Quarterdeck Restaurant** (25 Dock St., 11 A.M.–8:30 P.M. daily May–Oct.) by the harbor.

If all it would take to make you happy is some decent pizza, stop by **Fresh Pasta Shoppe** (206 Upper Main St., 508/627-5582, 11 A.M.–9 P.M. Mon.–Sat. and 4–9 P.M. Sun.) near the Triangle as you bike in or out of town. Right at the tip of the Triangle itself is **The Square Rigger Restaurant** (Edgartown–Vineyard Haven Rd. at Beach Rd., 508/627-9968, 5:30 P.M.–close daily year-round, $26–33), the family-friendly home of surf-and-turf at prices that turn locals into regulars. If you want to sample lobster, make this your first stop (VTA bus 1, 11, or 13).

Another of Edgartown's most affordable and dependable restaurants is **The Newes from America** (Kelley St., 508/627-4397, www.kelley-house.com, 11:30 A.M.–11 P.M. daily late May–early Oct., 11:30 A.M.–10 P.M. Mon.–Thurs. and 11:30 A.M.–11 P.M. Fri.–Sun. the rest of the year, closed Christmas, $7.50–11.95) in the Kelley House inn at the corner of N. Water and Kelley Streets. Lower prices don't mean inferior food—the Newes's family-friendly menu of soups, sandwiches, burgers, and dinner-sized salads keep the casual crowd happy, as does the great selection of microbrews (in bottles and on draught). On winter weekends it's the only place for miles that serves food till 11 P.M., so night owls take note.

Across the street, behind one of the porches of the rambling Colonial Inn (where Somerset

Maugham sat out World War II), **Chesca's** (38 N. Water St., 508/627-1234, www.chescasmv .com, 5:30–10 P.M. daily mid-Apr.–mid-Oct., $24–38) serves up fine Italian-influenced cuisine with a blend of paper-napkin informality and the hardwood, clapboard dignity of an old New England resort. The dining room's contented murmurs aren't due just to the catchy mood music—the food is inspiringly fresh, seasoned with a bold hand, and prettily garnished. The restaurant doesn't stint on the desserts, either, as anyone who believes "the more sugar, the better" will happily discover. Though many entrée prices are well over $30, there are some relatively good values on the menu, particularly among the pasta dishes.

When it's time to impress your traveling companion with a fine meal at a local hot spot with the see-and-be-seen crowd—maybe lobster and chanterelle crêpes, followed by seared cod on a porcini ragout in sugar snap pea broth, or garlic-crusted sirloin on white-bean-and-truffle fondue—make a beeline for **◖ Alchemy**

(71 Main St., 508/627-9999, www.alchemymv. com, 11 A.M.–2:30 P.M. Mon.–Sat. and 5:30– 10 P.M. daily late May–early Oct., dinner only hours vary Oct.–New Year's and Feb.–May, $27–32.50). It also serves a less expensive bar menu—$13 burgers and fries, $9 duck confit nachos, that sort of thing. In the off-season months, the bar is a fine place to discover how island life doesn't allow strangers to stay unacquainted for long.

Out-of-the-ordinary touches abound at **◖ Détente** (3 Nevins Sq., 508/627-8810, www .detentemv.com, 5:30–10 P.M. daily late May– early Sept., hours vary the rest of the year, $30– 36), a hidden gem behind the Colonial House. Here you might encounter summer peaches in a savory appetizer, autumnal parsnip pierogis paired with a rich osso bucco, Sardinian fregola to soak up the jus of a rack of lamb, tropical lychee contrasting with yellowfin tuna tartare. In short, more inspiration and flavor is packed into the dozen dishes served here than is found on many menus twice as long.

Up-Island

In a place that's already about as laid-back as New England gets, up-island is where the Vineyard truly goes barefoot and fancy-free. Yet the relative seclusion of the up-island villages have traditionally meant that they are the purview more of the summer resident or cottage renter (and celebrities seeking true rural privacy) than day-trippers or weekenders (despite the hordes of bus tourists flocking to the renowned Gay Head Cliffs). "Out of sight, out of mind" seems to be up-island's best disguise—trailheads look a lot like just more private driveways, their flora and vistas hidden from view. Visitors dedicated to maximizing beach time give scant thought to the up-island forests, and people who spend the big bucks to bring their cars across seem most likely to use them to avoid exercise rather than to explore the nooks and crannies where public shuttle- and tour-bus riders can't go. In short, for a va-

riety of reasons, even many up-island regulars never bother to explore the unheralded hilltops, ponds, and meadows virtually in their own backyard. All of which means that if you're able to spare the time and expense to get around up-island at your own pace, you have the chance to still discover the quiet, down-home place that for most down-island residents exists now more in memory than in fact.

WEST TISBURY

Oak Bluffs may boast greater diversity, but the most politically liberal town on the island is this 1896 splinter from next-door Tisbury. Familiarly known as "West Tis" (rhymes with fizz), the community had no qualms about allowing hippies to set up camps in the woods back during the first reign of bell-bottoms and the fringed halter. Even today, the area sets a standard for island liberals—in addition to the still-common colonial office of fence viewer, whose modern mandate is to arbitrate boundary disputes—for example, West Tis elects a Community Right-To-Know Committee, an EPA-mandated oversight group that most towns resist on the grounds that industry has only positive attributes.

Although this was one of the fastest-growing towns in the entire state during the go-go years of the 1980s, agriculture is still a vital part of West Tisbury's economy and landscape. From onions and lettuce to strawberries and cream, if you partake of an island-grown meal there's a good chance its components were cultivated here. Most of the upscale restaurants around the island make a point of using local produce wherever possible, but for a true taste of the Vineyard's truck gardens, look no further than the **West Tisbury Farmer's Market,** in and around **The Grange Hall** (sometimes still referred to as the "Old Ag Hall"), a picture-book 1859 Gothic Revival shingled and gabled barn on State Road in the town center. There are farm stands down-island, too (Edgartown's **Morning Glory Farm,** at the corner of Machacket Road and Edgartown–West Tisbury Road, about a mile from Main Street, is in a class by itself), but between mid-June and Columbus Day weekend, The Grange is *the* place to go, as much for the ambience as for the fruits of the earth. Along with purveyors of affordable vine-ripened tomatoes and enough cruciferous vegetables to make even the surgeon general happy, there are always a few vendors selling fresh-cut flowers, a few masters of the Mason jar selling pickles and preserves, a few bakers with homemade desserts, and even fresh-spun yarn from just-sheared sheep fleece. If you have someplace to store the leftovers—not that there are likely to be many—Eileen Blake's pies are deservedly legendary. Also famous are the fresh Vietnamese spring rolls by Thi Khen Tran, who sells copies of her cookbook, *The Egg Roll Lady of Martha's Vineyard,* too. The market is held on Wednesday afternoons 3–6 P.M. and Saturday mornings 9 A.M.–noon; needless to say, Saturdays are mobbed.

Up-island's other celebration of its agrarian lifestyle, August's annual **Livestock Show and Fair,** raises the rafters of the "New Ag Hall" with a Vineyard version of the standard county fair; expect oyster shucking contests and great live music along with those horse pulls and tables of homegrown or homemade food. Also known as the Fairgrounds, the new hall is on Scotchman's Lane about half a mile north of the old one.

Like a page of Norman Rockwell's sketchbook, the village around the farmer's market is exemplary 19th-century picket-fence New England, from the handsome Congregational Church and well-trod porch of Alley's General Store to the proper old homes on tree-lined Music Street. (This leafy residential way was once known to some as Cowturd Lane; "Their savage eyes turn'd to a modest gaze by the sweet power of music"—perhaps Tisbury residents renamed the street back in the 1800s for the piano-playing daughters of a resident whaling captain and six of his neighbors). Those old ivories are long silent but the visual arts live on, in and around **The Field Gallery and Sculpture Garden** (1050 State Rd., 508/693-5595 or 800/355-3090, www.fieldgallery.com, 10 A.M.–5 P.M. Mon.–Sat. and 11 A.M.–4 P.M. Sun. May–Dec.), next door to the Council on Aging center and wonderful town library. As at most other island galleries, exhibits here are condensed for the summer rush, so each Sunday evening is opening night for the new art of the week. If you can't wait around for the wine and cheese, **Back Alley's,** across the street, has a smart lineup of reasonably priced deli sandwiches and baked goods (try those snappy ginger cookies), plus dirt-cheap coffee refills for folks who supply their own cups.

Half a mile away, facing the end of Scotchman's Lane, is the large **Granary Gallery** (636 Old County Rd., 508/693-0455 or 800/472-6279, www.granarygallery.com, daily late May–early Oct., at least weekends in shoulder season Easter–Christmas), which has the distinction of being the Time-Life Gallery of Photography's sole New England representative. So, in addition to locally produced artwork in a variety of media (paint-

BRIAN JOLLEY

The "New Ag Hall" in West Tisbury hosts a variety of shows and fairs.

ing, sculpture, and sometimes textiles), you can browse—or buy—limited editions, mostly signed, of museum-quality prints by the likes of Alfred Eisenstadt, Margaret Bourke-White, Andreas Feininger, Carl Mydans, and others whose contributions to *Life* magazine have become some of the nation's most recognizable cultural images.

North Tisbury

Within 25 years of their arrival, the English outgrew their settlement at Edgartown and moved up-island to this fertile area between Priester's Pond and Lambert's Cove Road. It was known to the Wampanoag as "Takemmy" (place where people go to grind corn), but may actually be from *touohkomuk* (wilderness). The English shepherds called the settlement Newton (Edgartown then was Old Town), and later Middletown. Now named after the post office station sandwiched into a storefront within a small shopping plaza, this part of West Tisbury township no longer qualifies as very wild, although it's still plenty rural.

One part of the scenery worth stopping for is the **Polly Hill Arboretum** (809 State Rd., 508/693-9426, www.pollyhillarboretum.org, 7 A.M.–7 P.M. Thurs.–Tues. in season, dawn–dusk Thurs.–Tues. off season, suggested donation $5), about a half mile south of the junction with North Road (to Menemsha). Old stone walls are reminders that these 60 acres were once a sheep farm, but Ms. Hill, a famous horticulturist, turned a third of the property into an open-air laboratory for her work with ornamental trees and shrubs. The rest is kept in natural meadows and woods. Perhaps the most captivating time to visit is mid-June through July, when the dramatic allée of Kousa dogwoods is in full bloom, but there are numerous rare and beautiful species worth seeing throughout the year, as well as a variety of programs at the visitors center.

North Tisbury's commercial side includes a couple of arty shops along State Road, most notably **Martha's Vineyard Glassworks** (683 State Rd., 508/693-6026, www.mvglassworks .com, 10 A.M.–5 P.M. daily late May–early Oct.), where the art of shaping attractive, functional items out of molten glass is on view daily in season. It's also worth checking out the **Yes, We Have No Bananas Gallery** (455 State Rd., 508/696-5939, www.bananasgallery.com, 11 A.M.–6 P.M. daily mid-June–early Sept., closed Tues.–Wed. mid-Sept.–early Oct. and late May–early June, hours vary mid-Oct.–mid-May) for their unconventional clothing, jewelry, and gifts.

Christiantown

Although the Puritan founders of the Massachusetts Bay Colony had obtained their royal patent by promising that "the principall Ende" of their settlement was to convert the indigenous people to "the Christian Fayth," the evangelical magistrates in Boston were so busy prosecuting heretics and building a profitable mercantile trade that it was here on the Vineyard—outside their jurisdiction—that the first New England mission to the Indians began. The year after the Mayhews settled their parish in Edgartown, a Wampanoag named Hiacoomes became the island's first voluntary convert to Christianity. Within a decade, over 10 percent of the Vineyard's Indian population had signed a covenant with the proselytizing Thomas Mayhew, Jr.; within a generation, a majority of the Wampanoag on both the Vineyard and Nantucket had not only converted, but had also resettled themselves into a series of 15 Christian communities modeled after the English style, a move heralding the profound change colonization wrought upon both Wampanoag culture and the Indians' relationship to the land.

One such town stood in North Tisbury on what's now Christiantown Road, off Indian Hill Road. With the blessings of Thomas Mayhew, Sr., Wampanoag converts consecrated their first Christian church and burial ground here in 1659, on a parcel of land rented from a pair of up-island sachems. Besides the small number of descendants denied federal tribal recognition, all that's left of Christiantown now is tiny little Mayhew Chapel, an 1829 replacement of the original; the mostly unmarked tombstones opposite; and abandoned 19th-century cellar holes and stone walls along the peaceful loop trail through adjacent **Christiantown Woods Preserve.** About a 0.25-mile walk past the parking lot (follow the road and take the first right; this is not driveable) is a state-maintained **fire tower.** When the tower is staffed—which is only when fire danger is high—you are welcome to go up and enjoy the fine 360° views.

Chicama Vineyards

While most island farmwork happens far from the curious eyes of off-islanders, an exception exists here, at the state's first legitimate winery, which offers tours up to five times a day in season. Year-round, taste from a variety of red and white table wines made from European *vinifera* grapes, including chardonnay, zinfandel, cabernet, a cranberry dessert wine, and the occasional sparkling wine. Chicama also bottles its own line of gourmet flavored oils, mustards, vinegars, chutneys, and other condiments. All, like the wines, are for sale in the gift shop-tasting room (80 Stoney Hill Rd., 508/693-0309, hours vary in May, 11 A.M.–5 P.M. daily June–Christmas, Sat. only Jan.–Apr.). The winery and shop are a mile down sand-and-gravel Stoney Hill Road from the signposted turn off State Road.

CHILMARK

Sparsely populated Chilmark (whose year-round population is less than 850) once resembled a little corner of New Zealand, with more sheep than humans. The resemblance stopped at labor and farm expenses, though; before Down Under's huge sheep stations put the kibosh on profitability, back in the mid-19th century, Chilmark wool had been second only to whale oil in importance to the island economy. (The whalers themselves made use of the wool in the form of heavy-duty satinet coat fabric milled in neighboring West Tisbury.) Dozens of miles of drystone walls, all built from up-island's limitless supply of glacial till, lie half-hidden in the now-forested hills, quiet reminders of the loose-footed flocks of black-faced sheep that once dominated the local landscape. If you've taken a close look at these sorts of walls elsewhere in New England, you'll notice that the Vineyard has a distinctive "lace wall" in its repertoire—a rickety-looking style with big gaps between the stones. The usual explanation has been that these perforated walls were built to accommodate stiff ocean winds raking over the once-treeless up-island hills, but Susan Allport, author of the exceptional *Sermons in Stone,* suggests the design may be a Scottish import. Although there is no written record one way or the other, a nearly identical style of see-through stone wall in Scotland—called a Galloway dike—was built to look deceptively precarious specifically to frighten bold sheep from attempting to leap over them.

Despite having its trees and vegetation shorn to the ground by its early "husbandmen," Chilmark still boasts some of the island's best soil, even if these days artists and telecommuting professionals far outnumber local farmers (though farms still seem to outnumber retail shops). The center of the village is the intersection of State (alternately known in Chilmark as South Road), Middle, and Menemsha Cross Roads (named Beetlebung Corner, after the stand of tupelo trees whose hardwood was valued by ships' chandlers for making mallets—beetles—and cask stoppers—bungs). On the east side of the intersection is the **Chilmark Library** (508/645-3360, Mon.–Thurs. and Sat.), whose "Island Room" is an ideal rainy-day destination for anyone whose appetite has been whet by the morsels of history presented here. Also hard by the corner is the **Chilmark Store** (7 State Rd., 508/645-3739, deli 7 A.M.–7 P.M. daily May–mid-Oct., market stays open till 8 P.M.) a worthy pit stop for cyclists and others in need of a sandwich or slice of pizza. If your consumer impulse runs to something more stylish than groceries and minor housewares, check out the town's popular Flea Market, on the grounds of the **Community Church** (8:30 A.M.–3:30 P.M. Wed. and Sat., end of June–late Aug. or early Sept.), where mostly professional craftspeople, artists, and antiques dealers market seconds or blemished wares passed over by regular retail

buyers at prices which, while not a steal, are generally well-discounted.

With the exception of the village of Menemsha, most of Chilmark is rather leery of tourists. Summer's hordes may pay the bills but that hasn't alleviated the Not In My Back Yard syndrome. (If you've never thought of yourself as the vanguard of the great unwashed, just attend a local town hearing the next time someone proposes creating a public beachfront reserve, and listen to the dire predictions of how you'll ruin the neighborhood. You'd think tourists are just Hell's Angels in beach gear.) But not all Chilmark's inhabitants are loath to receive visitors; nothing's going to faze Lillian Hellman or John Belushi, for example, at their eternal residences in **Abel's Hill Burying Ground,** on South Road less than three miles from West Tisbury's town line. While they're probably the most famous tenants, anyone with an eye for good epitaphs and fine stone-carving will take greater interest in the many historic 18th- and 19th-century markers.

Menemsha

Anyone who wants proof that some of the people around here make a living off something besides the tourists can come to this Chilmark village and admire the Coast Guard station poised above the water in the golden light of a late summer afternoon. But the even bigger attraction is the fishing fleet in Menemsha Basin, whose catch ends up on tourists' plates all over the island. Watching guys in rubber boots shovel fish into barrels against a backdrop of buoy-covered shacks crowned with whale-shaped weathervanes is undeniably picturesque—especially compared to down-island's retail barrage—but it resists any use of the word "quaint." If this place is an anachronism, it's only because so much of the region no longer soils its hands with old-fashioned cash register keys or Touch-Tone telephones.

Besides watching sunsets framed by the boat basin's thicket of swaying masts, Menemsha's summer visitors come for hiking, swimming, and seafood in the rough. Cyclists looking for a shortcut to Aquinnah—and a chance to avoid some of the hills and punishing headwinds encountered on State Road—won't want to miss the **Menemsha Bike Ferry** (508/645-5154, $4 one-way, $7 round-trip), which shuttles across Menemsha inlet to West Basin, near the east end of Lobsterville Beach. It operates on demand daily 8 A.M.–6 P.M. July–Labor Day, plus weekends in the shoulder months of June, September, and October, weather permitting. But before you make a descent to the Menemsha inlet, check the signs at any of the approaches in Chilmark, West Tisbury, or Aquinnah to confirm whether the ferry is indeed running.

AQUINNAH

The most remote of the island's six towns, rural Aquinnah (year-round pop. 344) seems to stand in sharp relief against the fortunes of its sister communities. Although its population rebounded in the 1990s to keep pace with the rest of the Vineyard's double-digit percentage gains, Aquinnah has an unemployment rate nearly three times the statewide average, and the lowest average household income in all of Massachusetts. By the numbers, it would seem to belong in Appalachia rather than on one of New England's most star-studded resorts. The numbers, however, don't tell the full story. Most of the town's property owners are summer people whose incomes boost the statistics somewhere else—if their accountants let the government know about it at all. Many other residents thrive on an underground economy of cottage artisanship, cash contract work, or investment income that escapes the attention of labor statisticians. With vacant land selling for $200,000 an acre and town kids tending to go to prestigious colleges and graduate schools, Aquinnah might be called many things, but "poor" isn't one of them.

Along with Mashpee on Cape Cod, Aquinnah is one of two Massachusetts communities with a significant Native American population—almost 30 percent, according to the last national census. Most are Wampanoags of the Aquinnah (Gay Head) band, one of the remaining handful of the 50 or so bands that once made up the Wampanoag nation; descendants of two other bands, the Christiantown and Chappaquiddick, also live in the community, although their cultural identity hasn't been maintained well enough to receive the same recognition. If every tribal member lived in Aquinnah, they'd outnumber their non-Indian neighbors by more than four to one, but more than half of the 992-member band live off-island, and most of the rest live down-island.

In the 17th century, this area belonged to the sachemship Aquinnah (high land). Most of it stayed under Indian ownership until the 19th century, when condescending schemers pressured or duped native landowners into quite literally giving away the farm. After lengthy legal action, a few hundred acres were finally returned to the local Wampanoag after they obtained federal recognition in 1987, but there's no reservation—the restored acres came with some strings attached. Not surprisingly, accepting less than full control over a parcel of ancestral land much smaller than hoped for was a controversial price to pay for tribal recognition. During most of the 19th and 20th centuries, the community was known as Gay Head, after the high escarpment on which the lighthouse still stands, but in 1997 residents voted to return to their indigenous roots.

For anyone interested in the Wampanoags' history, the **Aquinnah Public Library** (State Rd. at Church St., 508/645-9552, 2–7 P.M. Mon., Wed., and Fri.; 10 A.M.–4 P.M. Sat.), has a room devoted to books about and by Native Americans. Ask the librarian to suggest a few of local relevance.

◀ Gay Head Cliffs

Declared a National Natural Landmark in 1966, 130-foot high Gay Head Cliffs have been a tourist attraction for as long as tourists have come to the Vineyard. Cliff-climbing is *definitely* off-limits—it's dangerous and accelerates the severe erosion of the unanchored clay—but you can admire the antediluvian strata from above or below, depending on whether you take

© KATHRYN OSGOOD

the eroding cliffs at Gay Head

a five- or fifty-minute walk from the parking lot. If the ground could talk, those multihued layers could tell some mighty interesting stories, if the fossilized remains of camels are any indication. On clear or partly cloudy evenings, the clifftop overlook provides exceptional front-row seats for watching the sun extinguish itself in the ocean off Rhode Island.

Adding to the photogenic view from the cliffs is the 19th-century red-brick **Gay Head Lighthouse** (508/645-2211), whose alternating red and white flashes warn ships away from Devil's Bridge, a treacherous line of partially submerged offshore rocks that prompted construction of the original 1799 beacon. Tricky currents and bad weather still sank many a sailing vessel on these rocks, even after the dim lanterns of old were replaced with the powerful Fresnel lens now seen in the yard of the Vineyard Historical Society; worst among these various disasters was the wreck of the *City of Columbus,* on which more than a hundred of its sleeping passengers died within a few minutes on a winter's night in early 1884.

Although the immediate grounds of the light are fenced off from public access throughout most of the year, on summer weekends (Fri.–Sun.) between June's solstice and September's equinox, the tower and grounds are opened for self-guided sunset tours ($3, free to children under 12, free to everyone on Mother's Day). The gates open 90 minutes before sundown and close 30 minutes after. Tours are canceled if the weather is so lousy that the sun can't be seen.

With the exception of a few tacky little gift sheds and fast-food stalls on the path to the clifftop overlook, Aquinnah is blissfully lacking in commercial attractions. Hungry visitors will find breakfasts, burgers, sandwiches, fried seafood, salads, and diner-style desserts at the seasonal **Aquinnah Restaurant** loftily perched at the cliff edge (Aquinnah Circle, 508/645-3867, 8 A.M.–3 or 4 P.M. daily mid-May–Columbus Day, 8 A.M.–7:30 P.M. daily late June–Aug., hours vary Easter–mid-May). Please note that despite the declared schedule of open hours, if business is too slow due to bad weather, the eatery may not remain open past 4 P.M. even in peak season.

ENTERTAINMENT

Modern dance is the bailiwick of **The Yard** (Middle Rd. off Beetlebung Corner, 508/645-9662, www.dancetheyard.org) an up-island artists' colony founded in the early 1970s and located in Chilmark, close to Beetlebung Corner. Their Barn Theater hosts a season of dance performances by colony residents at least one weekend a month from May to September, often including premieres of improvisational works that will next appear (at much higher prices) in New York City.

Real traditional New England **contra** and **square dances,** sponsored by the Country Dance Society (508/693-5627 or 508/693-9374), take place monthly off-season, September–May, at the Chilmark Community Center and West Tisbury's Grange Hall. Beginners are welcome; call for schedule and dates, or consult newspaper calendar listings.

RECREATION
Beaches

For the duration of summer, up-island towns restrict most of their beaches to residents or renters who bring a copy of their lease on a local house to the requisite office at town hall. Don't think the permits apply only to cars: Chilmark's beach attendants will check them no matter how many wheels—or feet—you come in on. (Guests of Chilmark B&Bs and inns can obtain walk-in beach permits, and can take advantage of the Chilmark beach shuttle bus that services the town's handful of lodgings; inquire at check-in.) So, **Lambert's Cove,** in West Tisbury; **Lucy Vincent** and **Squibnocket Beaches,** in Chilmark; and **Philbin** and **Head of the Pond** Beaches, in Aquinnah, are thus off-limits to most visitors from June through September—although at gorgeous Lambert's Cove, nonresidents are free to come catch the sun's last golden rays 6–9 P.M. But despair not—the publicly accessible alternatives are by no means negligible.

West Tisbury, for example, has a pair of conservation properties along the south shore whose mix of pond and ocean beaches amply reward the effort of reaching them. **Long Point Wildlife Refuge** (508/693-3678, 9 A.M.–5 P.M. June 15–Sept. 15, additionally 9 A.M.–7 P.M. Fri.–Sun. July–Aug., dawn–dusk otherwise, $3 for anyone over 15 plus $10 parking June 15–Sept. 15) another property of the Trustees, has half a mile of dune-backed beach along the Atlantic that rarely gets congested—thanks to the strict limit on the number of vehicles admitted. For more elbow room on hot, clear days, arrive early and walk west from the parking lot. To get there, turn off the Edgartown–West Tisbury Road onto Waldron's Bottom Road (look for the Trustees sign) and then follow the arrows.

Just west of Long Point is the Land Bank's **Sepiessa Point Reservation,** with a small beach along the edge of Tisbury Great Pond (watch for sharp oyster shells on the beach). The pond itself is a body of saltwater and marsh now hemmed in on the ocean side by barrier dunes (private) that are breached twice

© KATHRYN OSGOOD

A father takes his children fishing at Squibnocket Beach in Chilmark.

a year to maintain the pond's salinity, vital to maintaining its shellfish population. This place is virtually unknown even to most Vineyarders, so don't be surprised if you have it to yourself. Though free, parking is extremely limited; beachgoers should use the first trailhead pull-out and leave the southerly ones for folks who have boats to schlep. The walk to the beach from the upper trailhead is just over a mile, mostly through woods.

Menemsha Beach is Chilmark's most accessible—a big, family-friendly north shore spot with plenty of parking, food, restrooms, and views of the local fishing fleet returning to adjacent Menemsha Harbor; from the village center, follow signs for Dutcher Dock. A second, concession-free north shore beach—quite a lovely one, too—is found at **Great Rock Bight Preserve,** a Land Bank property quickly reached by a short trail accessed off of North Road; look for the Land Bank sign a little under four miles south of State Road. By contrast, the Land Bank's **Chilmark Pond Preserve,** off South Road opposite Abel's Hill

Cemetery, offers what's tantamount to a private beach club, with the lesser of 10 vehicles or 40 people allowed onto the property at any one time. The preserve's small piece of the south shore lies just east of permit-only **Lucy Vincent Beach.** Lucy Vincent is regarded by some as the island's finest beach, but don't get your hopes up—to even reach the ocean dunes, you must bring a canoe or kayak and paddle diagonally across Chilmark Pond (be sure to read the lengthy posted explanations of where you can and cannot land on the opposite shore). In the end, it's one plum that may stay tantalizingly out of reach, despite being free and public.

Arguably the best public swath of south shore surf and sand is at the Land Bank's **Moshup Beach** and adjacent **Aquinnah Public Beach,** just a scant half-mile or so from the famous Gay Head Cliffs. Limited parking is available—for a punitive $20 in summer—in the lot at the State Road loop atop the cliffs, near the public restrooms (where, incidentally, the down-island shuttle bus stops). Cyclists will find free racks down Moshup Trail at the beach itself.

East of the well-marked Land Bank property line is residents-only Philbin Beach; in the other direction, toward the base of the cliffs, is the island's principal nude bathing area. Up until the '90s, it wasn't uncommon to see people painting themselves from top to bottom with the richly colored clay from the cliffs, but enforcement of the prohibition against all climbing, digging, and souvenir-taking from this Wampanoag-owned National Landmark has been sharply increased in the years since. The strict rules are not the work of mere spoilsports—clay removal artificially hastens erosion. Simply walking around the base of the spectacular marine scarp, however, is perfectly legit.

Aquinnah's only other public shore is sheltered **Lobsterville Beach,** a mecca for surfcasters. The absolute ban on parking on Lobsterville Road makes access difficult, however. Aquinnah house renters and inn guests who obtain town parking permits (and the lucky few who snatch up the three or four spaces available for nonresidents) can park a mile away in the small lot at the end of West Basin Road, just across the narrow channel from the fishing boats in Menemsha Basin; otherwise, it's a two-mile walk from the Aquinnah bus stop up at the clifftop loop.

By far the best non-automotive approach is via the Bike Ferry from Menemsha, when it's operating (June–October). Of course, if it's swimming rather than fishing that you want, save yourself a mile walk or ride and stick to state-owned **West Jetty,** at West Basin; despite the protection from prevailing southwesterly winds, Lobsterville is generally much too rocky to stretch out a towel on (although it should be pointed out that the offshore eelgrass and crab beds aren't everyone's idea of tactile pleasure).

Kayaking

If you're serious about becoming a sea kayaker, you probably want to take lessons from a serious paddler committed to the sport, such as John Moore at **Kayaks of Martha's Vineyard** (508/693-3885, www.kayakmv.com). Two- to two-and-a-half-hour beginner's lessons ($35 per hour, plus $25 for a boat) cover all the basics—equipment, strokes, safety and rescue—but lessons are tailored to suit your skills. Though based at Lambert's Cove, John's business is mobile, so just phone to arrange an appropriate outdoor classroom. Off-season requests aren't a problem, either—he's a year-round resident, and even has dry suits for arctic souls who want to play in nippy April or November.

The Trustees of Reservations offers kayak tours of Tisbury Great Pond in summer.

Manuel F. Corellus State Forest

This forest was originally set aside to protect the dwindling population of the heath hen, a relative of the prairie chicken extinguished on the mainland through hunting and habitat loss. But the gesture was undermined by a big forest fire and continued hunting. By 1932, the hen was extinct. In spite of a legacy of tree farming, a blight that's killing off the remaining stands

Manuel F. Correllus State Forest

of red pine, and proximity to the island's airport, some trail-savvy islanders consider the state forest a hidden gem. Hikers interested in the Vineyard's floristic communities won't find any better place to sample the island's pitch pine barrens and scrub oak bottoms, for example—and mountain bikers can crisscross the forest on miles of fire roads. If you happen to visit during a snowy winter, you'll find good cross-country skiing through the property, too. Pick up a map and advice from the helpful staff at the forest headquarters (508/693-2540), off Airport Road.

◖ Long Point Wildlife Refuge

Big waves along an exceptional South Shore beach are the draw for summer visitors to this isolated up-island spot (508/693-3678, www .thetrustees.org, 9 A.M.–5 P.M. Mon.–Thurs. and 9 A.M.–7 P.M. Fri.–Sun. June 15–Sept. 15, dawn–dusk otherwise, $3 per person over 15 plus $10 parking June 15–Sept. 15, free otherwise). Bird-watchers and wild blueberry lovers may prefer the trails around the grasslands and shrub-

covered heath opposite the high-season parking lot on Long Cove Pond. Interpretive trail guides to the mile-long barrier beach-and-grassland loop are available year-round at the parking-lot bulletin boards, and are downloadable online. The other mile-long trail visits the freshwater marsh along the edge of Long Cove, where in spring and summer, you might hear frogs singing for sex, see herons stalking their supper, or spot river otters before they spot you.

Spring is also a good time to catch migrating ducks feeding on the ponds and songbirds scouting nesting sites in the woods. Fall is impossible not to enjoy—as the last papery pink salt-spray roses start to fold, the bayberry and huckleberry bushes impart a warm burgundy glow to the heathlands, and the waterfowl stop over again on their way south. On good summer swimming days, you'd do well to consider biking in to avoid being turned away when the parking lot fills; but off-season, this is a good place to be alone with your thoughts and brisk ocean breezes.

Naturalist-guided kayak tours of Tisbury Great Pond are offered in season (508/693-7392, 8:30 A.M., 11 A.M., and 1:30 P.M. daily June 15–Sept. 15, $25). Reservations for the 90-minute excursions are strongly recommended. For an out-of-the-ordinary paddling experience, sign up early for one of the special moonlight paddling tours offered over three or four nights preceding, during, and after the full moon (dates vary June–Sept., $45).

In summer the refuge gates are locked an hour after admissions end, so don't expect to hang around for watching the sunset over distant Aquinnah or admiring the star-studded carpet of the Milky Way.

Summer access is via Waldron's Bottom Road off the Edgartown–West Tisbury Road; follow the signs to the high-season parking lot by the beach (fresh water and restrooms available). Off season, the gate at road's end is closed; mid-September through mid-June, visitors should then use the heavily potholed, single-lane dirt track called Deep Bottom Road (again, follow the signs) to get to the facilities-free parking area near the caretaker's cottage.

© KATHRYN OSGOOD

Sepiessa Point Reservation

Like nearby Long Point, this Land Bank reservation protects some of the planet's last remaining acres of sandplain grasslands, backed by a large swath of woodlands along the edge of Tiah's (rhymes with wise) Cove, one of many slender inlets to Tisbury Great Pond. Since the only public boat access to the Great Pond is via the reservation's cove-side canoe and boat slides, most islanders familiar with this unheralded place know of it by the cove's name instead of the peninsula's. The property sports a short stretch of hard, sandy beach along the pond edge, too, but heed the posted warnings about the broken oyster shells, which are about as friendly to tender, unshod feet as discarded metal sardine cans. At a small pull-out near the reservation entrance—the only parking available to hikers and swimmers (each boat slide has its own handful of spaces)—a signboard identifies the trails that loop through pine-oak woods and converge on the grassy meadows about a mile away. Though quite plain for most of the year, the meadows are good wildflower territory in spring—the bushy rockrose, Nantucket shadbush, and other rare sandplain plants blossom throughout May and June. Summer's insects and autumn's berries bring birds out of the woods to forage throughout the rest of the high season, and if you look carefully before they all get eaten, at the end of summer, you may spot fruit-bearing creepers of the wild grapevine that supposedly inspired the island's name. Northern harriers, another of the state's rare species, have occasionally been sighted hunting in the meadows for rodents and insects.

Free year-round, Sepiessa Point is signposted with the Land Bank logo along Tiah's Cove Road, a dead-end fork off New Lane in West Tisbury. Only about 1.25 miles from the Edgartown–West Tisbury Road, the reservation is accessible to most bikes and even up-island shuttle riders who request a stop at New Lane, almost across from the volunteer fire station. A downloadable PDF of the reservation's trail map is available from the Land Bank's website, www.mvlandbank.com.

◖ Cedar Tree Neck

Ask your innkeepers or island hosts to recommend their favorite hiking spot and nine times out of ten they'll nominate this property of the Sheriff's Meadow Foundation. Located on West Tisbury's North Shore, it fully earns its reputation with nearly two miles of looping trails through woods, wetlands, and dunes; along a brook; along a morainal ridge; and along the beach. A kid-friendly pamphlet—available in the map kiosk at the parking lot—provides interpretive details on one trail; others are summarized on memoranda posted in the kiosk by the property managers. The trails were designed in part by Anne Hale, whose locally published book *From Moraine to Marsh: A Field Guide to Martha's Vineyard* is the best natural history companion for walks around the Neck.

Swimming is prohibited along the property's gorgeous Vineyard Sound shoreline, and a summer attendant enforces this restriction—part of the terms that made the land public. As is the case nearly everywhere on the Vineyard, neighboring houses are never far from sight, but the beauty of the Neck will put them clean out of your mind. In fact, don't be surprised if a scant half-hour of soaking up the views from the beach has you forgetting your *own* home. Located at the end of Obed Daggett Road, off Indian Hill Road, Cedar Tree Neck is free all year. A bike rack is provided, but restrooms aren't.

Waskosim's Rock Reservation

Straddling the West Tisbury–Chilmark town line near the headwaters of pristine Mill Brook are nearly 200 acres almost straight out of the 19th century: abandoned farmland bordered by dry-stone walls, the ever-encroaching forest, and wetlands that feed that brook, a vital tributary of Tisbury Great Pond. The waters of the brook are so clean that they're home to the brook lamprey, a species whose hypersensitivity to pollutants has made it widely endangered.

Presumably named after a local Wampanoag, Waskosim's Rock is a giant cracked boulder that marked a 17th-century boundary between

English and Indian lands. Natural forest succession has obscured the views once afforded from the rock itself, but fine down-island vistas may yet be found by the cleared fields rising out of the Mill Brook valley and from occasional breaks in the hilltop forest. Since much of the abutting private property is equally undeveloped, trails through the reservation's varied habitats are as good for bird-watchers as for anyone looking for a glimpse of Vineyard Haven's water tower. Conspicuous summer visitors include flickers, cuckoos, blue jays, and ovenbirds (in the dry oak forest at the southern, high end of the property); cedar waxwings, swallows, song sparrows, and white-eyed vireos (out on the old pastures); and northern parula warblers (around the scrubby red maple swamp near the trailhead).

The reservation's entrance, and parking for both bikes and cars, is signposted with a discreet Land Bank logo beside North Road a few hundred feet on the Chilmark side of the Chilmark–West Tisbury boundary.

Fulling Mill Brook Preserve

Although drivers on Chilmark's Middle Road will most likely miss its small trailhead parking lot, the relaxing half-mile walk through the Fulling Mill Brook Preserve is worth turning around for. The quiet, lazy trout stream grows garrulous and boulder-strewn as it runs through mixed hardwood forest down the shoulder of Abel's Hill, part of the morainal ridge that runs between Tisbury and Aquinnah. Shrubby savanna interspersed with oaks and a spot of wildflower-filled meadow occupy some of the slopes over the stream.

The brook takes its name from the mill that used its waters in the process of "fulling" cloth—making it heavier through shrinking and pressing—back in the 1800s. In the 1700s, several tanners treated hides in this neck of the woods, too. Today, decaying leaf litter and fresh breezes have replaced the tannic scent of curing leather. In summer, woodland songbirds abound along the brook's path, but proximity to those drier upland habitats means you're as apt to hear mourning doves and song sparrows as the quiet call of the whippoorwill.

While cars are limited to the Middle Road lot, cyclists can take advantage of a second bike rack, on South Road, at the preserve's lower end, beside an impressive stone and wrought-iron gateway.

Peaked Hill Reservation

Three of the island's highest points, including Radar Hill, an old World War II garrison site, and 311-foot Peaked (PEA-kid) Hill, crown a cluster of ridges whose slopes were once nearly girdled with luxury homes. The Land Bank's timely acquisition of these Chilmark heights preserved some especially good vantage points for Aquinnah sunsets, views over the Elizabeth Islands to the Southeastern Massachusetts coast, and hawk-watching. Numerous large moss- and lichen-covered glacial erratics, chunks of granite gouged out of mountains or exposed bedrock farther north and deposited here during the last ice age, dot the wooded trails. Some of the stones form the panoramic ledges; others are distinctive enough to have their own names (such as Wee Devil's Bed) or serve as reminders of the late 18th- and early 19th-century farmers who cleared much of this land (their pin-and-feather technique for splitting huge boulders into gateposts and foundation slabs is writ large on the edges of unused stones).

The military has also left some marks here. They're mostly steel-and-concrete tower footings and broken asphalt, but notice, too, the mature tree grown up through the old Radar Hill fencing, its trunk indelibly tattooed by the rusty chain link. The reservation now plays host to a large herd of white-tailed deer, whose distinctive bite can be seen in the severed ends of lower branches on small trees and shrubs all over these 70 acres. The rich forest understory and dense thickets also provide vital cover for numerous small mammals and birds, including an array of finches, sparrows, swallows, warblers, and woodpeckers. Conspicuous but locally uncommon species such as yellow- and black-billed cuckoos, killdeer, and bluebirds have been sighted here, and the relatively high elevations attract red-winged hawks and

American kestrels during both breeding and migration seasons.

The entrance turnoff is signposted on Tabor House Road, a half mile from Middle Road. Parking, maps, and a bike rack are located eight-tenths of a mile up the potholed dirt lane—always take the right fork, or you'll have to back out of several private driveways.

Menemsha Hills

Part of the reason the vista from the shoulder of Peaked Hill is so attractive is that the wooded hills bordering Vineyard Sound on the other side of North Road are protected by the Trustees' Menemsha Hills Reservation. Several miles of trails offer walkers oak tree shade, hilltop views, and bracing winds along the lip of the 150-foot marine scarp over Vineyard Sound. Ruminate over the landscape, where sheep once grazed within the property's drystone walls; watch birds gorge themselves on the heath's summer berry crop; or pretend you're Thomas Hart Benton, the Missouri-born painter who summered here in Chilmark for 56 years, and stroll the rocky beach (no swimming!) with an artist's eye for the play of light and water upon the rough coast. In late fall or winter, you might spot harbor seals basking on the rocks or bobbing in the surf offshore.

A Trustees' white-on-green sign marks the reservation's parking lot off North Road in Chilmark, a little over half a mile west of the junction with Tabor House Road. Admission is free.

ACCOMMODATIONS

Up-island may not offer a large quantity of lodging choices, but it certainly has a wide variety, including the island's only hostel, a number of traditional home-style B&Bs, a luxurious inn built around a 1790 farmhouse, and modern lodgings built in the 1970s. Prices, however, are concentrated at the low and high ends, with a big gap between them.

Under $50

The Vineyard's only true budget accommodation is West Tisbury's **Hostelling International**

Martha's Vineyard (525 Edgartown–West Tisbury Rd., 508/693-2665 or 888/901-2087, www.usahostels.org, mid-May–early Oct., $32–35 HI members, nonmembers add $3), a rambling, cedar-shingled Cape-style structure at the edge of the state forest on an isolated stretch of the Edgartown–West Tisbury Road. For anyone unfamiliar with the concept, many hostels now offer private rooms for families and couples, but when this one was designed, in the 1950s (it's the first American youth hostel built specifically for the purpose), the prevailing ethic called for stacking hostelers like kids at summer camp—20 or more per room. So until someone endows this fine old place with a massive capital renovation budget, its big, bunk bed–filled dorm rooms, slightly rustic common spaces, and woodsy locale will remain the archetype of hostel life—especially when the huge downstairs bunk room is filled by some exuberant school group.

The bottom line is that when all 78 beds are full, it's a bit zoo-like, despite the staff's superhuman efforts. Off-season, it's one of the most welcoming—and well-run—hostels in the business. Advance reservations are absolutely essential in summer, and highly recommended off-season.

Although accessible by bike path, car, and summer shuttle buses, the hostel is three miles from the nearest decent market, so if you plan to use the spic-and-span kitchen, you may want to shop ahead for groceries. Internet access is available.

$50-100

Up-island's epicenter of affordability is West Tisbury, where nearly half the lodgings belong to various descendants of old Thomas Mayhew himself—few of whom seem interested in fleecing visitors. The price leader of the year-round lot is **The House at New Lane Bed & Breakfast** (44 New Lane, 508/693-4046, housenl@vineyard.net, $85 d cash only, $20 more for one-nighters in season) on seven attractive acres just off the Edgartown–West Tisbury Road, offering three rooms, all with shared baths.

$100-150

Writers searching for inspiration may particularly appreciate the creative vibes around **The Cleaveland House** (620 Edgartown–West Tisbury Rd., 508/693-9352, criggs@vineyard. net, $85 s or $100 d cash only) at the corner of New Lane, home to the author of a series of mysteries set on the Vineyard. The circa-1750 house is chock full of character, with lots of family heirlooms and stories to tell, and plenty of cozy places to kick back and think up excuses for your editor after the surrounding acres' beauty distracts you from your muse. In addition to a small room for singletons there are two fireplace-equipped rooms, one a king and the other with two twin beds. Please note, none of these rooms has a private bath, and there's a two-night minimum in season.

Just across the road, **The Red Hat B&B** (629 Edgartown–West Tisbury Rd., 508/696-7186, www.theredhat.com, $100–115 d cash only) has three modest yet comfortable rooms, all sharing a bath. Like its neighbors, it also features a large yard, so after your island adventures you can relax on the sunny deck or in the hammock under the trees.

$250-350

Set way back in the woods at the end of a sandy lane off upper Lambert's Cove Road, West Tisbury's **◖ Lambert's Cove Country Inn** (90 Manaquayak Rd., 508/693-2298 or 866/526-2466, www.lambertscoveinn.com, mid-Mar.–early Dec., $225–355 d, two-room suite $550) exudes informal sophistication. Fifteen guest rooms are spread among the buildings of what was once a grand residential country estate. The original 18th-century farmhouse, barn, and carriage house have all been completely renovated from the cellar to the rafters to create a secluded oasis of thoroughly modern comfort amid expansive, beautifully landscaped grounds. No two rooms are alike, but the warm palette and tasteful fabrics they have in common would be right at home on the cover of *Elle Decor*. Oriental carpets on hardwood floors here, four-poster and canopied feather beds there, a lot of private decks, marbled baths, abundant pillows, flat-screen TVs with DVD/CD players—you get the picture (and if not, visit their website for photos of every room). This popular inn also features an all-weather tennis court, a modest outdoor swimming pool, and passes to lovely Lambert's Cove Beach (beach umbrellas and chairs provided). Complimentary made-to-order full breakfasts are served in the inn's restaurant, which happens to be one of the island's best choices for dinner, too.

The **Menemsha Inn & Cottages** (12 Menemsha Inn Rd., 508/645-2521, www .menemshainn.com, May–Oct., $280–350 d, cottages and houses $2,700–4,600 per week) offers a wide range of lodging options from modern motel-style rooms with two queen beds to houses that comfortably sleep six. It sits on 14 hillside acres—including a pasture with resident cow—above the cute little village of Menemsha, just off Chilmark's North Road immediately south of the Menemsha Cross Road junction. Contemporary in design and decor, the inn offers a choice of 15 well-appointed doubles and suites, 12 one- and two-bedroom, fully equipped housekeeping cottages, and two three-bedroom houses, nearly all facing Vineyard Sound. Rates include a complimentary self-serve breakfast of cereals and baked goods. If you have a group, the Carriage House's six ocean-facing suites and large two-story common room with big cushy sofas around a stone fireplace would serve as an ideal home base. Take advantage of the on-site fitness center, game room, playground, or tennis court, or take the path at the bottom of the hill to the public beach in Menemsha, 500 yards away. Beautiful sunset views of Aquinnah and Menemsha Bight, luggage-saving extras such as beach chairs and umbrellas, and guest passes to Chilmark's exclusive town beaches (regular shuttle bus service provided in season) make this a deservedly popular place, despite the absence of any air conditioning (fans are provided). Book early. Peak rates last from mid-July through August, dropping about 15 per cent for the three or four weeks before and after, and by about a third for the first and last four weeks of the season.

$350 and Up

Just through the trees bordering the Menemsha Inn, under common ownership but managed separately, is **The Beach Plum Inn** (50 Beach Plum Ln., 508/645-9454 or 877/645-7398, www.beachpluminn.com, May–Oct., $325–450 d), with 11 rooms between its main house and three adjacent bungalows. The decor is a modern mix of solid summery colors paired with printed fabrics and flocked valances, and some rooms feature whirlpool tubs and private decks or patios. The seven landscaped acres include a regulation-size croquet lawn. Guests can use the gym and tennis court next door, and also have the pick of Chilmark's beaches, from the public one a short walk down the hill to permit-only Lucy Vincent and Squibnocket beaches a short shuttle-bus ride away on the Vineyard's south shore. A complimentary full gourmet breakfast is offered at the inn's restaurant, also highly regarded for its evening fine dining.

FOOD

Despite having a hostel full of them in its midst, the rural end of the Vineyard is not very kind to budget travelers. The foot-thick topsoil seems to yield not only fresh produce, but fancy destination dining. Next to nothing stays open past Thanksgiving out here, and most places start paring back their days and hours after September. Also remember that all three up-island towns—West Tisbury, Chilmark, and Aquinnah—are dry, so stop first at an OB or Edgartown package store if wine is vital to your dining pleasure.

Up-island's only reasonably priced eating is almost exclusively takeout. Worthwhile grocery-store deli counters include **Garcia's Bakery & Deli at Back Alley's** (1045 State Rd., 508/693-8401, noon–5 P.M. daily, year-round, $6–13) and **Fiddlehead Farm** (632 State Rd., 508/696-6700, 11 A.M.–3 P.M. Mon.–Fri., 11 A.M.–5 P.M. Sat.–Sun., year-round, $4–9) in West Tisbury, and **The**

oysters from a crab shack on the beach in Menemsha

Chilmark Store (7 State Rd., 508/645-3739, 10 A.M.–6 P.M. daily year-round, $7–8) at Beetlebung Corner.

In Menemsha, a pair of small summer-only shacks draw patrons from across the island, each with its own passionate following. For fried whole-belly clams and other shellfish, visit **The Menemsha Bite** (29 Basin Rd., 508/645-9239, www.thebitemenemsha.com, 11:30 A.M.–3 P.M. daily, May–June and Sept.–Oct., 11 A.M.–9 P.M. daily, July–Aug., $8–16), on the road to Dutcher Dock and the village beach.

For juicy burgers and soft-serve ice cream, check out **The Galley** (515 North Rd., 508/645-9819, noon A.M.–8 P.M. daily year-round, $8–18), at the edge of Menemsha Channel. You can also dine for under $20 at the gift shop–eatery on the top of the Gay Head Cliffs, but come for the view, not the food.

Inquire after the best lobster on the Vineyard, and residents will most often steer you to **Larsen's Fish Market** (56 Basin Rd., 508/645-2680, 11 A.M.–6 P.M. daily

May–Oct., $13–19) in the heart of Menemsha. This is a taste of New England, deliciously unadorned. As the name makes clear, it's not a restaurant, but call ahead and order a lobster and they'll boil it for you on the spot to eat out back on the lobster traps at the edge of the dock, at one of the picnic tables nearby, or right on the beach. A variety of seafood soups and snacks are prepared daily, too, such as crab cakes, lobster bisque, seafood chowder, spicy stuffies (chorizo-stuffed clams), and seafood salad from the refrigerated cases inside the door. An al fresco picnic of Larsen's sweet tender fresh lobster chased down by steaming chowder as flavorful as fine bouillabaisse and fragrant as the sea, while the sun sets slowly into the ocean and keening gulls wheel in the evening breeze, is an ambrosial experience not soon forgotten.

Other prime up-island restaurants offer innovative, upscale cuisine in settings that range from studiously casual to stylishly contemporary. Several are found on the premises of the elegant inns tucked into the woods, such as West Tisbury's **Lambert's Cove Country Inn** (90 Manaquayak Rd., 508/693-2298, www.lambertscoveinn.com, 5:30 P.M.–close

daily mid-June–mid-Sept., hours vary but at least Thurs.–Sat. mid-Apr.–New Year's Eve, $28–40). Conservative-sounding fare—roast chicken, filet mignon, poached lobster—is paired with rich accompaniments, such as salt cod ravioli, apple Madeira wine reduction, and wild mushroom ragout, such that each dish deliciously exceeds the sum of its attractively presented parts. (Too bad they don't serve tea of comparable quality.)

Plenty of island flavor—Caribbean island, that is—runs through Chilmark's **@ the Cornerway** (13 State Rd., 508/645-9300, www.atthecornerway.com, 6 A.M.–close daily late May–Sept., $28–45), a stone's throw from Beetlebung Corner. The chef-owner, Deon Thomas, puts an Anguillan spin on local ingredients. As visitors to that British West Indies hotspot know, this means gourmet preparations with eye-catching presentation and bold flavors. Seafood has a starring role, of course—mussels flambeed with rum, cod cakes with Scotch bonnet guacamole, swordfish with sweet potato fries—but carnivores will also find plenty of tantalizing choices, from steak and duck to traditional Carib favorites like jerk chicken and braised goat.

Festivals and Events

MAY

Ancient pagans helped wake up the earth from its winter slumbers with community rituals on the first of May. Find out for yourself how effective parading around a Maypole can be at shaking off the waning grip of cold weather by joining in the **May Day Celebration** at the Native Earth Teaching Farm (94 North Road, Chilmark, 508/645-3304). A potluck dinner is held following the afternoon of festivities, so bring along something to contribute if you plan on staying until sundown.

JUNE

Midmonth, sup like royalty at **A Taste of the Vineyard Gourmet Stroll,** on the Dr.

Fisher House lawn behind the Old Whaling Church in Edgartown (508/627-4440, www .mvpreservation.org, $125). Proceeds from this food, wine, and beer blow-out, extravagantly catered by some 70 island restaurants and fine food purveyors, benefit the Martha's Vineyard Preservation Trust.

On the 16th, celebrate **Bloomsday** at Vineyard Haven's Katherine Cornell Memorial Theater, with a night of music, drama, and recitations inspired by James Joyce's *Ulysses* (www .artsandsociety.org, $15).

JULY

In the middle of the month, yachties swarm the Vineyard to race in the **Edgartown Regatta,** sponsored by the Edgartown Yacht Club (508/627-4364, www.edgartownyc.com).

During the second weekend of the month the **Annual Island Scoop Ice Cream Festival** (St. Augustine's Church, 84 Franklin Street, 508/693-7917) helps participants beat the heat with cool treats.

The third weekend brings a flavor of the Vineyard's Portuguese heritage to Oak Bluffs in the form of **The Feast of the Holy Ghost** (Vineyard Ave., 508/693-9875, www.mv holyghost.com), held both outdoors and at the Portuguese-American Club.

AUGUST

The first Monday of the month finds philanthropic islanders congregating under a big tent on the grounds of Outerland, a nightclub on the airport's entrance road, in order to take part in the **Possible Dreams Auction** (508/693-7900, www.possibledreamsauction .org, $25). High rollers bid on the opportunity to dine, play golf, go sailing, play tennis, or enjoy other private backstage encounters with Vineyard "dreammakers," including many A-list celebrities. Proceeds benefit M. V. Community Services, an island-wide social service agency.

For four days ending the third weekend of the month, the Martha's Vineyard Agricultural Society sponsors its annual **Livestock Show and Fair** (508/693-4343, http://mvas.vineyard. net, $8) at the West Tisbury Fairgrounds (also called the Ag Hall), with old county fair–style fun, replete with games, contests, good food, and music.

SEPTEMBER

The first Saturday after Labor Day, Edgartown's non-profit FARM Institute holds their annual fundraiser, **Corn-A-Palooza** (Aero Ave., 508/627-7007, www.farminstitute.org,

4–8 P.M., $15). Enjoy foot-stompin' live music, hayrides, games for kids, a giant corn maze, organic burgers and hot dogs, and of course, fresh corn on the cob.

On the second Saturday after Labor Day, Oak Bluffs takes its final bow of the season with **Tivoli Day** (508/696-7463), named for a once-grand but now long-gone Victorian dance hall. Circuit Avenue, closed to all traffic, is filled with a day-long street fair, including a parade, music, food, raffle tables, and such contests as the Waitperson Olympics, in which waiters and waitresses compete in carrying containers of water without spilling.

NOVEMBER

The day after Thanksgiving is traditionally reserved for America's national shopping spree. Locally this tradition translates into the annual **Vineyard Artisans' Holiday Festival** (Ag Hall in West Tisbury, 508/693-8989, www.vineyardartisans.com, 10 A.M.–4 P.M., $2), where a cornucopia of locally made crafts tempts browsers into buying something for everyone on their holiday gift-giving list. The entrance fee goes to the local high school's scholarship fund.

DECEMBER

Hardy year-round residents stoke the spirit of the holidays with Vineyard Haven's annual **Chowder Contest,** on the first Saturday of the month (508/693-1151) and **Christmas in Edgartown,** on the second weekend of the month (508/627-9510).

On New Year's Eve, Vineyard Haven celebrates **Last Night, First Day** (508/693-0085, www.mvy.com), with arts performances throughout the afternoon and evening, capped off by fireworks over Vineyard Haven Harbor at 10 P.M.

Information and Services

BANKS AND ATMS

You won't ever be far from an automated teller machine in the down-island towns, but up-island is a different story—beyond Beetlebung Corner, there's nothing. The deplorable practice of charging fees for cardholders who don't have local accounts infiltrated the Vineyard even before it took hold of the rest of the state, so count on being charged for remotely accessing your money.

Those using foreign currency must make their cash exchanges prior to arriving—none of the banks here handle such transactions.

MEDIA AND COMMUNICATIONS

For the most up-to-date arts and entertainment suggestions, check out Thursday's *Martha's Vineyard Times*, which includes nightclub live music listings in its calendar of events. Last-minute yard sales and estate auctions, on the other hand, are more likely to be found in the classifieds of Friday's more patrician *Vineyard Gazette*, regarded as one of the finest small-town newspapers in the nation—and possibly the most quaint. Its oversized page, aphoristic masthead, and columns devoted to bird sightings all betoken a bygone era in journalism.

On the radio dial, **WMVY-FM, 92.7,** is the local gentle pop and rock station and the best up-to-the-minute source for local beach and ferry reports. *All Things Considered* junkies who can't leave NPR behind, even while on vacation, can tune in the Vineyard's own community public radio station, **WCAI-FM, 90.1,** an affiliate of WGBH in Boston. Fans of freeform community radio should tune into the feisty local low-power non-commercial station, **WVVY-FM, 93.7,** "radio for the people," dedicated to the rich local music scene plus a dose of Amy Goodman's "Democracy Now" newscasts mixed in every weekday. Although this station's 93-watt transmitter limits audibility to the down-island towns, you can also catch its global beat, blues, psychedelarrythmia, and other shows streaming live from www.wvvy.org.

The Vineyard's own **Plum TV** (Channel 76), part of a national network of resort-based cable access stations, is an engaging source for catching up with current island events, interviews with islanders, and other local-interest stories.

If you like to peruse racks of promotional flyers or want more accommodations to choose from, drop in on the **Martha's Vineyard Chamber of Commerce,** on Beach Road in Vineyard Haven, opposite the fire station. Place an order from their website (www.mvy .com) or call ahead (508/693-0085) for a free copy of their visitors' guide. In high season, staffed information booths in all three down-island towns (marked on the relevant close-up maps) are able to give directions, provide dining and lodging information, and answer most general tourist questions. Edgartown's booth also sells postcards and stamps, accepts mail, and vends snacks.

PUBLIC RESTROOMS

The only year-round restrooms open to the public are at the Steamship terminal in Vineyard Haven and the Church Street Visitors Center in Edgartown. In summer, a number of other facilities open up all over the island: in the parking lot next to Vineyard Haven's Stop & Shop market, at the Steamship dock and on Kennebec Avenue in Oak Bluffs, at South Beach in Edgartown, in West Tisbury's Grange Hall on State Road, and at the bottom of the loop drive atop Gay Head Cliffs. Showers are also available (for a fee), at the bathhouse beside Oak Bluffs Harbor and the Manor House Health Club in downtown Vineyard Haven, next to the Chamber of Commerce.

MEDICAL EMERGENCIES

For speedy clinical care of illnesses and minor injuries **Vineyard Medical Services** (611A

State Rd., 508/693-4400), opposite Cronig's Market, accepts walk-in patients weekdays 9 A.M.–noon. For medical emergencies the island's full-service 24-hour medical center, **Martha's Vineyard Hospital** (One Hospital Rd., 508/693-0410, www.mvhospital.com), is located off Beach Road at the foot of East Chop about 1.5 miles equidistant from both downtown Vineyard Haven and downtown Oak Bluffs.

Getting There and Around

In summer, all three down-island towns are connected to the mainland by ferries and to each other by shuttle buses and paved bike paths. Here the great concentration of food and lodging, mostly within walking distance of each other and transportation, makes it entirely practical (even eminently sensible) to arrive without a car.

PUBLIC TRANSIT

Year-round island-wide public transportation is provided by the **Martha's Vineyard Regional Transit Authority** (VTA, 508/627-9663, www.vineyardtransit.com). It's entirely possible to visit every village on the island, connect to the Steamship docks in Vineyard Haven, get to town—any town—from the airport, and ride to the beach, all via one of the VTA's dozen different routes. Most of the buses run on a fixed hourly schedule, although off-season some routes have less frequent service (and the trolley to South Beach is only seasonal). In summer—from the third Saturday in June to the end of the Labor Day holiday weekend in early September, to be exact—systemwide frequency of service increases significantly. For instance, buses start rolling between the three down-island towns at 6 A.M., with half-hourly service from around 7 A.M. until after midnight, and service every 15 minutes from 10:30 A.M. until 6:45 P.M. All fares are $1 per town, including the town of origin—i.e., $2 between towns, and $3–4 for full cross-island rides. One-, three-, and seven-day passes for unlimited travel are available from the drivers or at the Edgartown Visitors Center on Church Street for $6, $15, or $25, and monthly, yearly, and school-age student passes are available, too, although only from the Edgartown Visitors Center. Cyclists who underestimate the strength of the island's headwinds will be gratified to know that all VTA buses have bike racks mounted on the front.

Two of the VTA routes provide nearly continuous service mid-May through mid-September to their respective downtowns from free peripheral parking lots on State Road in Vineyard Haven, by the Triangle in Edgartown, and at the Edgartown elementary school on West Tisbury Road.

BIKE RENTALS

Vineyard Haven, Oak Bluffs, Edgartown, and parts of West Tisbury are linked by more than 15 miles of paved bike paths, so cycling around the island is a snap even for riders normally intimidated by traffic. The only major portion of the island lacking segregated bikeways is the southwest corner, but the beautiful tree-canopied roads there make for lovely riding nonetheless. And what better way to work off those calories from last night's dinner?

Over a dozen shops rent bikes—three on Circuit Avenue Extension next to Oak Bluffs' ferry docks, three within a block of Vineyard Haven's Steamship terminal, two within a stone's throw of Edgartown's central Main Street–Water Street intersection, and a couple more at the Triangle on Upper Main Street in Edgartown. Guests of B&Bs and inns away from the town centers can take advantage of the free bike delivery and pickup offered by such outfits as **Martha's Bike Rentals** (Lagoon Pond Rd., in Vineyard Haven, opposite the post office, 508/693-6593, Apr.–mid-Nov.); **Vineyard Bike & Moped** (next to the

© KATHRYN OSGOOD

You can rent bikes for the day or week from Edgartown Bicycles.

Strand movie house in OB, 508/693-6886); or **Wheel Happy** (S. Water St. in Edgartown, opposite the Harborside Inn, 508/627-5928, Apr.–mid-Nov.). Most rental fleets are trendy mountain bikes and hybrids, but retro three-speeds, tandems, lighter road bikes (perfectly adequate if you intend to stick to pavement), and trailers for towing kids are also widely available. (Wheel Happy caters to corporate outings with fully guided cycling tours from Edgartown to Oak Bluffs, too.)

If you've brought your own wheels and need repairs, several rental shops double as fix-it stops: Vineyard Haven's year-round **Cycle Works** (105 State Rd. next to Cronig's Market, 508/693-6966); **Anderson's Bike Rental** (Circuit Ave. Ext. in OB, 508/693-9346); **Edgartown Bicycles** (212 Upper Main St., 508/627-9008); or **R. W. Cutler Edgartown Bike Rentals** (1 Main St., 508/627-4052 or 800/627-2763, Apr. 1–Nov. 1).

TAXIS

For island-wide convenience, choose from among the many available taxi companies.

Since each town has its own set of regulations for taxi companies based within their borders, fares vary somewhat from one company to the next, particularly when it comes to the extras—fees for extra passengers, luggage, pets, late-night drop-offs, and driving on dirt roads. So if the same cab ride you took yesterday ends up suddenly costing more today, don't jump to the conclusion that you're being gypped.

Rates for up to two people from the Steamship docks in either Vineyard Haven or OB can run as high as $50–60 to Aquinnah, $18–20 to the hostel in West Tisbury, and $10–17 between down-island towns. Additional passengers are usually $3 each, and in the timeframe of 1–7 A.M. expect the fare to be doubled.

Taxi Services
Vineyard Haven
All Island Taxi, 800/693-TAXI or 508/693-2929, www.allislandtaximv.com
Harbor Taxi, 508/693-9611
Patti's Taxi Service, 508/693-1663
Stagecoach Taxi, 508/627-4566 or 800/299-5411, www.mvstagecoachtaxi.com
Tisbury Taxi, 508/693-7660

Oak Bluffs
Atlantic Cab, 508/693-7110, www.atlantic cabmv.com
A BIG Cab Company, a.k.a. Marlene's Taxi, 866/693-8294 or 508/693-0037, www.mar lenestaxi.com
Martha's Vineyard Taxi, 866/688-2947 or 508/ 693-8660, www.marthasvineyardtaxi .com
Your Taxi, 508/693-0003 or 800/396-0003

Edgartown
Accurate Cab, 508/627-9798
Adam Cab, 508/693-3332 or 800/281-4462, www.adamcab.com
Bluefish Taxi, 508/627-7373
Jon's Taxi, 508/627-4677

West Tisbury
Mario's Taxi, 877/627-6972 or 508/693-8399

CAR AND MOPED RENTALS

If you're staying down-island in summer, you really want to avoid driving. You may not think so, as you imagine all the luggage you have to carry and all the shopping you want to do—but if it's a vacation you're after, seriously consider your determination to drive; you're letting yourself in for a slow, stop-and-go crawl through intersections packed with 20,000 other cars, not one of which will yield to your left turn. If you're coming in the off-season or intend to spend most of your time up-island and have never ridden a bicycle, driving is a slightly better idea. Just mind all those cyclists, and the deer at night—particularly on curvy, shoulderless up-island roads.

If you decide to rent a car, be prepared for rates that fluctuate wildly. Ever-popular Jeeps and convertibles that rent for over $170 a day on any midsummer holiday, for instance, may drop by half off-season unless the weather is spectacular and demand is strong. Don't expect anyone but the major chains to quote prices over the phone—the independent operators prefer not to commit to anything that may scare off potential business. Remove any diamond jewelry you may be wearing and don't introduce yourself as a doctor, and you'll find these indie outfits are prepared to haggle—so long as you're mellow and not too pushy, and they can see that the competition across the street still has a car or two in the lot. By the way, before you pay a massive premium for renting one of those macho four-wheelers, remember that driving on Vineyard beaches is restricted to privately owned vehicles with valid permits. Oversand vehicle permits for Chappaquiddick are $160 from the Trustees (508/627-7689); for Norton Point—the only other part of the Vineyard's coast open to off-road vehicles—the requisite permits are $80 from the Treasurer's Office (9 Airport Rd., 508/696-3845), or at South Beach in the summer.

Car Rental Agencies
Vineyard Haven
A-A Island Auto Rentals, Five Corners, 508/696-5300 or 800/696-0233
Adventure Rentals/Thrifty Rent-A-Car, 19 Beach Rd., 508/693-1959

Beach Road Rentals, 95 Beach Rd., 508/693-3793
Budget, 36 Water St., 508/693-1911 or 800/527-0700

Oak Bluffs
A-A Island Auto Rentals, 31 Circuit Ave. Ext., 508/696-5211
Budget, 12 Circuit Ave. Ext., 508/693-1911 or 800/527-0700
Sun-N-Fun Jeep Rentals, Lake Ave., 508/693-5457

Edgartown
AAA Island Auto Rentals, 196 Main St., 508/627-6800 or 800/627-6333
Auto Rentals of Edgartown, 141 Main St., 508/627-7241

Airport
A-A Island Auto Rentals, 508/627-6800
Budget, 508/693-1911 or 800/527-0700
Hertz Rent-A-Car, 508/693-2402 or 800/654-3131
Thrifty Rent-A-Car, 508/696-0909 or 800/367-2277

HITCHHIKING

Despite the rips summer congestion is rending in the fabric of the Vineyard's small-town life, the island has a well-deserved and enviable reputation as a great hitchhiking spot, a small vestige of the 1970s preserved here thanks to the large proportion of pickups and sport utility vehicles and the island's small size (no need to worry about making conversation for just a couple of miles). If you've never tried thumbing a ride, this is a good place to start; if you mourn the passing of safe hitching in the rest of the U.S., you'll find this a welcome time warp. Which isn't to say you shouldn't trust your instincts; if you aren't comfortable with someone who's stopped to offer a lift, decline the ride. Since the preservation of this casual anachronism depends on visitors as well as residents, don't think that just because you don't know your way around, you aren't eligible to contribute—if you have extra capacity in your car, share it.

MOON MARTHA'S VINEYARD

Avalon Travel
a member of the Perseus Books Group
1700 Fourth Street
Berkeley, CA 94710, USA
www.moon.com

Updaters: Michael Blanding and Alexandra Hall
Editor: Elizabeth Hollis Hansen
Series Manager: Kathryn Ettinger
Copy Editor: Maura Brown
Graphics and Production Coordinator:
    Domini Dragoone
Cover Designer: Domini Dragoone
Map Editor: Kevin Anglin, Mike Morgenfeld
Cartographers: Chris Markiewicz, Jon Niemazyk,
    Jon Tweena

ISBN-13: 978-1-59880-410-2

Text © 2009 by Jeff Perk.
Maps © 2009 by Avalon Travel.
All rights reserved.

ABOUT THE AUTHOR

Jeff Perk

Author and photographer Jeff Perk has swum with giant mantas in Micronesia, sweated through a Bolivian silver mine, gone dog-sledding in Finland, sipped slivovitz in Hvar, enjoyed the Takarazuka in Tokyo, and, as a result, has never needed to own a TV. He grew up in southern Illinois, catching fireflies, eating fresh catfish, and smelling sweet magnolia blossoms in spring. He traded it all for fried clams and fall foliage when he left the humid prairie to attend high school and college in New England. After sampling life on the West Coast, briefly laboring in San Francisco's film industry, Jeff rebounded east in time to be swept up in Boston's high-tech boom of the late 1980s.

Despite racking up oodles of frequent flyer miles on business, Jeff's true travel addiction didn't strike until he crossed paths with an international cadre of globetrotters traipsing through New Zealand and Australia. A three-month sabbatical between jobs in 1989 grew into nearly four years of backpacking around South America, hitching rides aboard yachts in the South Pacific, and squeezing through slot canyons in the American Southwest.

As the mileage awards began to run out, it seemed only natural to become a travel writer — a job that allowed Jeff to embrace everything from scuba diving in Fiji to touring the backwater sloughs of the Mississippi Delta. During the latter half of the 1990s, Jeff finally sat still long enough to write the Moon Handbooks to his adopted city (Boston) and state (Massachusetts). He has also contributed to other guidebooks, including *Road Trip USA* and *Road Trip USA: New England*, and is editor of the 10th edition of *Car-Free in Boston*, the nation's oldest transit-users' guide. A periodic contributing editor for *Yankee* magazine, Jeff has also been published in newspapers and online.

When not writing about his latest adventures or selling his services to local software firms, Jeff can be found bouncing to the salsa beat of Jamaica Plain, Massachusetts, or online at www.jeffperk.com.